"A LITERARY FELLOWSHIP"

RELATIONSHIPS AND RIVALRIES
IN 19TH-CENTURY AMERICAN
LITERATURE

2] [Thomas Sinclair (lithographer)]; Pierre Duchochois (photographer). *Our Great Authors, A Literary Party at the Home of Washington Irving.*

"A LITERARY FELLOWSHIP"

RELATIONSHIPS AND RIVALRIES IN 19TH-CENTURY AMERICAN LITERATURE

by

SUSAN JAFFE TANE &
GABRIEL MCKEE

THE GROLIER CLUB
NEW YORK
2017

*Catalogue of an exhibition held at the Grolier Club
from November 16, 2017 –January 13, 2018.*

COVER IMAGE:
Thomas Hicks (artist), Alexander Hay Ritchie (engraver).
Authors of the United States (item 1).

A guide to the authors pictured on the cover and frontispiece
appears on pages 132–133.

Photography by Robert Lorenzson, New York.

ISBN: 978-1-60583-072-8

INTRODUCTION

In 1987 as I was walking through The International Fine Art & Antiques Show at the Park Avenue Armory I was inexplicably drawn to a book. Not just any book, but an 1845 first edition of *The Raven and Other Poems* by Edgar Allan Poe. The excitement accompanying this purchase was overwhelming. I caressed it in awe and wonder, completely amazed that a layperson such as myself could own such a treasure. That was the day I became a "Collector."

I had recently bought a New York City pied-à-terre and coincidently decided to transform the dining room into a library sitting room. I moved in, surrounded by bookshelves that were empty except for my one small, thin book standing alone. Eventually I moved many of my better books from my overflowing Long Island shelves, but my beautiful *Raven* continued to look forlorn. The bestselling novels, reference books and paperbacks looked out of place on the same shelf as *The Raven*. This book was no ordinary object: it warranted respect, and I wanted my library to reflect it. I dreamed of forming a "Collection" that I could immerse myself in, as well as to adorn my shelves, but I really didn't know how to begin.

I spent much time anguishing over the right and wrong way to collect, although it turns out there really isn't a wrong way. I considered acquiring the "high spots" of history, science, and literature to create a Gentleman's Library emulating Thomas Jefferson's. I pictured myself in the overstuffed corner armchair, drink in hand, savoring every book. But the truth is, I didn't want to read or reread Copernicus, Dante or Plato. My love was nineteenth-century American literature.

I decided to focus my efforts and resources instead on a single author and make that collection "important." Since I already had a copy of *The Raven* and loved Poe's work, it was natural to make Edgar Allan Poe, the man and his work, my focal point. But as with many collections, they tend to meander and take in peripheral material and ephemera. Poe, a harsh literary critic, reviewed the writers and poets of his day, so the next logical step was to branch out and collect choice items related to his contemporaries. I began to acquire the most important and rare pieces by the likes of Twain, Melville and Whitman, initially without a focused direction. Before too long I began to discover that I was most drawn to pieces that illustrated the relationships between these authors, and the broader literary world of editors and publishers. One of my first and favorite letters was written by Poe to Washington Irving, requesting a "blurb" for a forthcoming book. It reads:

> Now, if, to the very high encomiums which have been lavished upon some of my tales by these & others, I could be permitted to add even a word or two from yourself, in relation to the tale of "William Wilson" (which I consider my best effort) my fortune would be made. I do not say this unadvisedly—for I am deliberately convinced that your good opinion, thus permitted to be expressed, would ensure me that public attention which would carry me on to fortune hereafter, by ensuring me fame at once.

Another favorite is an 1875 letter by Mark Twain on literary piracy that hangs in my dining room. Clemens thanks "a respectable Boston publisher" for informing him about a man named Greer who was attempting to pirate some Mark Twain materials:

> Gentlemen: I thank you very much for exposing this man Greer's projects to me. He is a common thief . . . All of my stuff is amply protected, & none of it for sale—as Mr. Greer shall find to his serious cost the first time he closes a trade for any of it. I am exposing this filthy thief in to-morrow's Courant. If he will only carry out his word & call upon me he shall need assistance to get off the premises again.

It is precisely interpersonal gems like these that convinced me to ask my gifted librarian, Gabriel Mckee, to co-author this book accompanying the exhibition, "A Literary Fellowship." His special knowledge and skill is displayed as he weaves the intricate and revealing thread between these authors and their publishers. It is our hope that in reading these letters and exploring the stories behind these books, you will come to understand better the web of connections that supported the great authors whose words live on today.

ACKNOWLEDGEMENTS

Thanks to my booksellers, Stephan Loewentheil of The 19th Century Rare Book and Photograph Shop, Pom Harrington of Peter Harrington Rare Books, Kevin MacDonnell of MacDonnell Rare Books and Jim Cummins of James Cummins Bookseller. I trusted their guidance and good sense in helping me shape and enhance this esoteric collection.

Thanks to the Carl A. Kroch Library at Cornell University, and especially to Katherine Reagan, for allowing me to borrow back the manuscripts relating to Herman Melville that I donated a few years ago.

Thanks also to Richard Austin and Selby Kiffer of Sotheby's, and its Vice-Chairman Emeritus, David Redden, who were always available to offer sage advice and encouragement.

For their assistance with the editing of this catalog, thanks to George Ong, Karen Karbiener, and Julie Carlsen.

Fame and Public Persona in 19th-Century Literature

T HROUGHOUT the early nineteenth century, a culture of celebrity was developing in America. Increasing rates of literacy led to an explosion in popular press readership and a democratic demand for American voices. The spread of lyceums created a circuit for authors to speak publicly. P. T. Barnum's traveling shows created a new and sensationalist language for promotion. The development of photographic techniques extended the degree to which authors could be known to their audiences: the celebrity photography of public gallerists like Matthew Brady fostered "emotional intimacy . . . between the famous and their audience."[1]

With the combination of these factors, it was no longer enough for authors to simply write. Instead, they now needed to cultivate a public persona. Literary style, physical appearance, modes of dress and speech, and any personal details that found their way into the gossipy editorial columns of the popular press were all essential elements in a successful author's public identity. Audiences were eager to encounter authors as complete individuals, and by the middle of the century, "the American market was awash with celebrity memoirs and biographies, each putting forward a famous individual to be the object of public scrutiny."[2] It is no surprise that authors like Mark Twain and Walt Whitman carefully fashioned their public personae to attract an audience or embody an ideal—or that the reclusive Emily Dickinson withheld from publishing her poems at all,

1. Leo Braudy, *The Frenzy of Renown: Fame and Its History* (New York: Oxford University Press, 1986), 494.
2. David Haven Blake, *Walt Whitman and the Culture of American Celebrity* (New Haven: Yale University Press, 2006), 44.

refusing to make her private life public and leaving her words alone as an inheritance to her future audience.

In this new culture of celebrity, the portrait was a primary point of contact between artist and audience. Photographic portraits circulated widely as *cartes de visite* sold by photographers and distributors, but were also reproduced for publication by painters, engravers, and lithographers. Some artists delighted in the combination of multiple portraits into single scenes, creating an often-imaginary personal connection between authors. Others idealized their subjects—depicting them as either paragons of poetic virtue or tortured outsiders—or caricatured them, thus further reinforcing the elements of a celebrity's public persona. In this increasingly visual culture, authors' own words served to reinforce how the public viewed them: Poe successfully represented himself as a sort of aristocrat, utterly convincing admirers like Baudelaire.[3] Twain so thoroughly identified his image with cigars that a tobacco brand was named after him.

4] [Samuel L. Clemens]. Compton Label Works. "Smoke the Popular Mark Twain Cigars Sold Everywhere" advertising signage.

Autograph collectors sought an even more personal connection to notable figures of the nineteenth century, writing to request signatures and handwritten fragments from well-known authors. These requests could become a nuisance: Longfellow signed as many as seventy autographs in a single day, and in his later years Whitman used autograph requests as kindling in his wood stove.[4] Poe turned an analytical eye to the signature in his several essays on "autog-

3. Braudy, *The Frenzy of Renown*, 486.
4. Horace Traubel, *With Walt Whitman in Camden, Vol. 4: January 21 to April 7, 1889*, ed. Sculley Bradley (Philadelphia: University of Pennsylvania Press, 1953), 351–52.

raphy," which sought to describe the character of various notables through analysis of their signatures. These early attempts at handwriting analysis aside, a simple autograph renders its writer anonymous, separated from any context or content of thought. Autograph poems or prose reveal more of their authors. But some authors' signatures nevertheless represent character or connection, be it that of Oliver Wendell Holmes, who embellished his responses to multiple autograph requests with the identical stanza from his most famous poem, "The Chambered Nautilus"; or the single card with which one collector collected the signatures of three authors, creating an unlikely connection, over a span of five decades, between Washington Irving, Edward Everett Hale, and Mark Twain. In cases like these, an autograph becomes another form of self-representation in this era of growing literary celebrity. The fame exemplified by these portraits and autographs represents the most important form of literary fellowship: that between author and reader.

PUBLIC IMAGE LIMITED: PORTRAITS
OF AMERICAN AUTHORS

1] THOMAS HICKS (artist), ALEXANDER HAY RITCHIE (engraver). *Authors of the United States.* New York: [William P. Wright?], 1866. Hand-colored engraving, 23″ x 37⅛″.

2] [THOMAS SINCLAIR (lithographer)]; PIERRE DUCHOCHOIS (photographer). *Our Great Authors, A Literary Party at the Home of Washington Irving.* New York: Whitman & Co., 1865. Albumen print, 11⅛″ x 16⅞″, mounted on card, 16″ x 21″.

A notice in the April 1857 issue of the Crayon described a patriotic series of portraits commissioned by William P. Wright:

> Four artists of this city have been commissioned by Wm. P. Wright, Esq., to paint each a picture to form a series representing respectively the Artists, Men of Science, Literary men, and Merchants of our country. Mr. [George A.] Baker will paint the Artists; Mr. [Daniel] Huntington, the Savans; Mr. [Thomas] Hicks, the Literary characters; and Mr. [Thomas] Rossiter, the Merchants. The paintings, when finished, will be exhibited and engraved. The size of each canvas we believe is to be 9 by 14 feet. The commission is a very liberal one, and certainly a very creditable one to Mr. Wright.[5]

Wright died in 1866, prior to the completion of the series: only Rossiter's portrait of the merchants (now at the New-York Historical Society) and Hicks's canvas of authors (surviving only as an engraving by Alexander Hay Ritchie) were completed.[6]

Hicks's monumental portrait shows a gathering of forty-four American authors, among them Edgar Allan Poe, Washington Irving,

5. "Sketchings." *The Crayon*, vol. 4, no. 4 (April 1857), p. 123.
6. For a detailed history of the Wright Commission and Hicks's portrait in particular, see Letha Clair Robertson, "The Art of Thomas Hicks and Celebrity Culture in Mid-Nineteenth Century New York." Dissertation (University of Kansas, 2010), p. 74–106. Online. < https://kuscholarworks.ku.edu/handle/1808/7734 > (accessed February 24, 2016).

William Cullen Bryant, Harriet Beecher Stowe, Lydia H. Sigourney, Henry Wadsworth Longfellow, Oliver Wendell Holmes, Ralph Waldo Emerson, and others. Pride of place is given to James Fenimore Cooper, who stands at the center of the image. Overlooking the gathering in the background is a trio of European literary forebears, represented by portrait sculptures: Shakespeare, Goethe, and Dante.

The engraving was published in 1866, and was offered a few years later as a premium for subscribers to the *Independent*, as indicated by an 1872 solicitation notice signed by its publisher, Henry C. Bowen: "This is certainly the most beautiful and most valuable premium ever offered in the country for one subscriber . . . This wonderful picture always attracts attention and admiration and is well worth five times the price named—to say nothing of the value of The Independent which goes with it."[7]

Between the 1857 announcement in the *Crayon* and the publication of Hicks's engraving, other artists were inspired by the concept of an imaginary literary gathering. In 1863 Christian Schussele made an oil painting based on a drawing by Felix O. C. Darley depicting a fanciful gathering of "Washington Irving and His Literary Friends at Sunnyside."[8] The image was published as an engraving and circulated widely, spawning an imitation by the lithographer Thomas Sinclair in 1865.[9] Those pictured in both images include Irving, James Fenimore Cooper, Nathaniel Hawthorne, Oliver Wendell Holmes, Ralph Waldo Emerson, N. P. Willis, Henry Wadsworth Longfellow, and William Cullen Bryant. Both leave out female authors, though writers like Harriet Beecher Stowe were certainly well known enough to merit inclusion. Similar to the Hicks print, Ameri-

---

7. Quoted in Lance Schachterle, "Graphic Representations of Cooper." *The Writings of James Fenimore Cooper*, Feb. 13, 2008, < http://www.wjfc.org/picture.html > (accessed February 24, 2016).
8. Christian Schussele, "Washington Irving and his Literary Friends at Sunnyside." Oil painting, 1864. National Portrait Gallery, Object no. NPG.82.147. http://npg.si.edu/object/npg_NPG.82.147 (accessed May 17, 2017); Thomas Oldham Barlow, "Irving and his Literary Friends." Engraving, 1864. National Portrait Gallery, Object no. NPG.67.89. http://npg.si.edu/object/npg_NPG.67.89 (accessed May 17, 2017).
9. Thomas S. Sinclair, "Our Great Authors." Lithograph, 1865. National Portrat Gallery, Object no. NPG.78.23. http://npg.si.edu/object/npg_NPG.78.23 (accessed May 17, 2017).

can literature's debt to England is represented in both images by a bust of Shakespeare in the background. J. Gerald Kennedy notes that these images depicted New York and Boston-based authors side-by-side, ignoring the traditional rivalry between the two cities' authors; Irving himself had made his "anti-New England prejudices" clear in works like his *History of New York*.[10]

The overall composition of Sinclair's lithograph follows Darley and Schussele, but the individual figures seem to be based on a number of different sources. For example, the image of Washington Irving is based on painter Alonzo Chappel's individual portrait of him, while N. P. Willis (at the far right) is depicted in a pose matching that in one of his *carte de visite* photographs. As well as circulating as a lithograph, Sinclair's image was also issued in its present form, an albumen print by photographer Pierre Duchochois.

3] [UNIDENTIFIED ARTIST OR ARTISTS]. *Twenty Fine Steel Plate Engravings of Eminent Authors and Poets, With Fac-Similes of their Autographs*. [N.p.: ca. 1879–1890].

This souvenir set of authors' portraits includes both American and British authors, all of them male. Among those represented are Edgar Allan Poe, William Cullen Bryant, Ralph Waldo Emerson, Fitz-Greene Halleck, Lord Byron, Charles Dickens, and William Shakespeare. Other copies of this set bear the New York imprint of the German-born lithographer Ralph Trautmann, absent from this copy.

4] [SAMUEL L. CLEMENS]. Compton Label Works. "Smoke the Popular Mark Twain Cigars Sold Everywhere" advertising signage. St. Louis, [ca. 1877–85].

Beginning with the selection of his *nom de plume* at the beginning of his newspaper career, Samuel L. Clemens carefully crafted his public image, and in many respects he was far more successful as a

10. J. Gerald Kennedy, "Inventing the Literati: Poe's Remapping of Antebellum Print Culture," in *Poe and the Remapping of Antebellum Print Culture*, ed. J. Gerald Kennedy and Jerome McGann (Baton Rouge: Louisiana State University Press, 2012), 30–31.

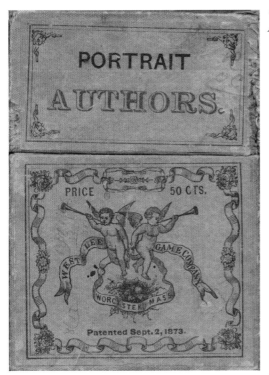

7] West & Lee. *Portrait Authors* card game, 1874.

NOVELISTS.

NATHANIEL HAWTHORNE.

Charles Dickens.
William Wilkie Collins.
William M. Thackeray.

NOVELISTS.

NATHANIEL HAWTHORNE.

This author is everywhere justly regarded as not only one of the finest descriptive writers of this age but one of the most original and analytical novelists of any preceeding age. He was born at Salem, Mass., July 4, 1804, and died at Plymouth, N. H., May 19, 1864. His early life was spent on a farm. He graduated at Bowdoin College in the famous class of 1825,—three of whom are among our present list of distinguished American Authors. In 1837, he collected the larger portion of his magazine and newspaper stories, and published them under the title of "Twice Told Tales." In 1843, he married and removed to the 'old manse' at Concord, which adjoins the first battle field of the Revolution, from which one of his books takes its name, "Mosses from an Old Manse." For several years he was connected with the Custom House at Salem, on retiring from which he published, "The Scarlet Letter," a powerful romance of early N. E. life, "The House of Seven Gables," "Blithedale Romance," the "Life of Franklin Pierce," (his old college friend, who afterward appointed him U. S. consul at Liverpool,) "The Marble Faun," etc.

celebrity than a businessman. Though his largest business ventures, such as investing in the ill-fated Paige Compositor and launching subscription publishing house Charles L. Webster & Co., ended in bankruptcy, he was arguably the biggest literary celebrity to date. The use of the name and face of "Mark Twain" for advertising purposes is a key component of Clemens's fame. Wisconsin cigar manufacturer Ed Aschermann registered a trademark for Mark Twain-branded cigars in 1877,[11] and this sign is the earliest known piece of cigar advertising to bear his name and image.

5] [SAMUEL L. CLEMENS]. Joseph Keppler. *Mark Twain: America's Best Humorist*. Lithograph portrait. "Puckographs," New Series, Number 1. Issued with *Puck*, December 16, 1885.

Austrian-born cartoonist Joseph Ferdinand Keppler founded the humor magazine *Puck* in 1871. Keppler was an expert caricaturist, as shown in this image of Mark Twain delivering a humorous lecture. Images such as this helped cement the place of Clemens's public persona in the popular imagination.

6] SAMUEL L. CLEMENS. Autograph letter signed ("Saml. L. Clemens") to an unidentified Boston publisher. Hartford, Conn., June 21, [1875]. Two pages on a single folded leaf of embossed stationary, 6⅞″ x 4½″.

> June 21.
> Gentlemen:
> I thank you very much for exposing this man Greer's projects to me. He is a common thief. He is the same chap who gets up the notorious blackmailing biographies of leather-headed nobodies. All of my stuff is amply protected, ~~too.~~ & none of it for sale — as Mr. Greer shall find to his serious cost the first time he closes a trade for any of it.
> I am ~~pi~~ exposing this filthy thief in to-morrow's Courant. If he will only carry out his ~~promise~~ word & call upon me he shall need assistance to get off the premises again.
> Thankfully Yours
> Saml. L. Clemens.

11. "Trade-Marks Registered During the Week." *Official Gazette of the United States Patent Office*, v. 12, July 24, 1877, p. 139.

Farmington Avenue,
Hartford.

June 21.

Gentlemen:

I thank you very much for exposing this man Green's praject(?) to me. He is a common thief. He is the same chap who got up the notorious black-mailing biographies of leather-headed me.

bodies. All of my stuff is amply protected, & none of it for sale — as Mr. Green shall find to his cost the first time he shall try to close a trade for any of it. I am exposing this filthy thief in to-morrow's Courant. If he will only carry out his word & call upon me he shall not hesitate to get off the premises again.

Thankfully yours,
Saml L. Clemens

PLATE 1.
6] Samuel L. Clemens. Autograph letter signed to an unidentified Boston publisher, June 21, [1875].

The Arrow and the Song.

—

I shot an arrow into the air;
It fell to earth I knew not where;
For so swiftly it flew, the sight
Could not follow it in its flight.

I breathed a song into the air;
It fell to earth I knew not where;
For who hath sight so keen and strong
That it can follow the flight of song?

Long, long afterward, in an oak
I found the arrow still unbroke;
And the song, from beginning to end,
I found again in the heart of a friend.

Henry W. Longfellow.

March 15. 1881.

PLATE 2.
21] Henry Wadsworth Longfellow. Autograph manuscript, "The Arrow and the Song."

For Twain, part of establishing his brand meant vigilantly guarding his copyright. Literary piracy was common in the nineteenth century, particularly because there was no international legal treaty protecting American authors from having unauthorized editions of their works published overseas. (By the same token, there was no such law protecting foreign authors from American pirates—meaning it was much cheaper for an American printer to pirate a foreign work than pay an American author for an original one). Twain was careful to secure British copyright for his works by having them issued in England before their release in America—usually only preceding the American edition by a matter of days. Nevertheless, Twain's works were frequent targets of piracy: for example, the second book appearance of "The Celebrated Jumping-Frog of Calaveras County" was an unauthorized printing in *Beadle's Dime Book of Fun* no. 3, and cheaply produced editions of his works were frequently issued by Canadian printers.

In this letter (see plate 1), Twain thanks an unidentified Boston publisher who informed him of a pirated edition of his works being offered for sale by a man named Greer. The specific edition being offered, and Greer's full name, are not mentioned. Twain followed through on his promise to "expose this filthy thief," and his letter on the matter appeared in the Hartford *Courant* on June 25, 1875.[12]

7⎤ WEST & LEE. *Portrait Authors* card game. Salem, Mass.: West & Lee Game Company, 1874. Boxed set of 64 cards.

This matching-based card game was first published in 1861 by G. M. Whipple and A. A. Smith under the title "Authors."[13] The 1874 edition issued by West & Lee was the first to include Mark Twain,

12. Samuel L. Clemens, letter to the Editors of the Hartford *Courant*, June 21, 1875 (UCCL 13001). *Mark Twain Project*, 2010, < http://www.marktwainproject.org/xtf/view?docId=letters/UCCL13001.xml;style=letter;brand=mtp > (accessed April 6, 2017).
13. The Strong, "Portrait Authors Card Game," The Strong: National Museum of Play, 2016, < http://www.museumofplay.org/online-collections/3/41/107.2718 > (accessed August 12, 2016).

alongside James Russell Lowell, Henry Wadsworth Longfellow, Oliver Wendell Holmes, Henry Ward Beecher, George Bancroft, and others. (Twain is categorized among "Humorists," rather than "Story Writers" or "Novelists.") Parker Brothers began issuing their edition of the game in 1875, and new editions of it are available from several publishers to this day.

8⌉ [SAMUEL L. CLEMENS]. HENRY WILLIAM BRADLEY & WILLIAM HERMAN RULOFSON, photographers. *Men of Mark*. San Francisco: Bradley & Rulofson, 1876. Cabinet photograph, 4¼″ x 6½″.

This composite photograph by San Francisco photographers Bradley & Rulofson unites 110 separate portraits, combined into "a galaxy of persons of distinction on the Pacific Coast, also, embracing many persons of note who have visited California since 1849," including politicians, explorers, authors, and entrepreneurs—all male. Among those pictured is Samuel Clemens, who moved to San Francisco in 1864, working as a newspaper reporter, primarily for the *Alta California;* he was photographed by Bradley & Rulofson in April 1868. An 1878 catalog of prominent figures photographed by the studio includes over 2,500 individuals, including politicians, clergy, actors, and artists; Twain is listed among the members of the "Newspaper Fraternity."[14]

9⌉ A. SHUMAN & CO. *Eminent Poets and Authors*, folio pamphlet. Boston: A. Shuman & Co., June 1892.

Abraham Shuman emigrated to the United States from Germany at the age of 11, and in 1869, at the age of 30, founded a clothing store in Boston. The firm did well, and the location of its elaborate building at the corner of Summer and Washington Streets in Boston came to be known as "Shuman Corner." In 1892, the store issued this commemorative broadside celebrating American and European authors. The tabloid-size publication includes portrait engravings,

14. Bradley & Rulofson, *Bradley & Rulofson's Celebrity Catalogue*. San Francisco: Printed by B. F. Sterrett, 1878, p. 25.

brief biographical sketches, and excerpts from the work of over two dozen authors, including Edgar Allan Poe, William Cullen Bryant, Henry Wadsworth Longfellow, and Ralph Waldo Emerson. A. Shuman & Co. was sold to Jordan Marsh in 1922, and the Shuman Corner store was expanded into a three-block, five-building complex. Jordan Marsh was sold in 1996 to Macy's, and a department store still stands at the original Shuman Corner site.[15]

10⌉ W. L. HASKELL. *Our American Poets.* [Chicago: Beckley-Cardy], 1903. Lithograph print, approximately 10″ x 29½″.

In the early twentieth century Chicago-based artist W. L. Haskell produced a number of lithographic banners commemorating authors, artists, and other prominent figures. This banner contains portraits of six poets: Will Carleton, Edgar Allan Poe, J. Whitcomb Riley, Eugene Field, Walt Whitman, and Bret Harte. Other lithographs in the series include "Great Musicians," "American Authors," "Women of the Bible," "Our American Statesmen," and an additional image of six more of "Our American Poets." Though lacking from this banner, other prints in this series bear the imprint of Beckley-Cardy, a Chicago-based distributor of educational supplies, indicating that the entire series may have been intended for use in the classroom.

11⌉ [GROLIER CLUB]. Edith Woodman Burroughs. Bronze medallion portrait of Edgar Allan Poe. New York: Grolier Club, 1909. 6¾″ diameter. One of 277 copies

12⌉ [GROLIER CLUB]. V. D. Brenner. Bronze medallion portrait of Ralph Waldo Emerson. [New York: Grolier Club, 1909]. 7¼″ diameter. One of 300 copies.

15. Bruce Allen Kopytek, "Jordan Marsh Company, Boston, Massachusetts," *The Department Store Museum*, September 2010, http://www.thedepartmentstore-museum.org/2010/09/jordan-marsh-company-boston.html (accessed January 24, 2017).

13] [GROLIER CLUB]. John Flanagan. Bronze plaque portrait of Henry Wadsworth Longfellow. New York: Grolier Club, 1911. 7½″ x 5¾″. One of 300 copies.

Between 1892 and 1911, the Grolier Club issued a series of five relief portraits of American authors. Issued in editions of between 173 and 372 copies in bronze and three copies of each in silver, the plaques were distributed to members of the club. Some of the artists who designed these portraits are best known for other idealized portraits of famous Americans: V. D. Brenner is best known for designing the Lincoln penny (first issued the same year as his Emerson medallion), and John Flanagan designed the Washington quarter twenty years after his Longfellow plaque.

14] BARRY MOSER. *Twelve American Writers*. [Easthampton, Mass.]: Pennyroyal Press, 1974. No. 6/50, one of ten copies issued for patrons of the project, bound in full leather with an extra suite of prints.

Early in his career, master engraver Barry Moser issued this portfolio of author portraits through the Pennyroyal Press. The collection, issued in an edition of fifty copies, includes stylized wood-engraved portraits and accompanying quotations from James Fenimore Cooper, Ralph Waldo Emerson, Nathaniel Hawthorne, Edgar Allan Poe, Henry Thoreau, Herman Melville, Stephen Crane, Mark Twain, Ernest Hemingway, William Faulkner, F. Scott Fitzgerald, and John Steinbeck. The authors selected for this project show the changing tastes of readers: Poe and Melville in particular had struggled to find an appreciative audience in their own day, but became far better known in the generations following their deaths.

"I BREATHED A SONG INTO THE AIR": MANUSCRIPT POEMS & PROSE

15] WILLIAM CULLEN BRYANT. Manuscript poem, "A Song for New Years' Eve." New York, [n.d.]. 1 page, 9⅞″ x 7⅞″. Framed with a cabinet photograph of Bryant.

Though his works are less well known today than those of contemporaries like Poe and Melville, William Cullen Bryant was one of the most popular authors of his day. "Song For New Year's Eve," composed in 1857 (more than three decades after his 1823 collection of *Poems* established his reputation), first appeared in *Harper's Magazine* in January 1859. The poem has received little critical attention, and is decidedly a minor effort. Yet in its lines we see hints of Bryant's friendships:

> Dear friends were with us, some who sleep
> Beneath the coffin-lid:
> What pleasant memories we keep
> Of all they said and did!

A brief, positive notice of the poem appears in the book *The Sunny Side of a Shut-In's Life* by Belle Ackison: "Now, do you not think that worth reading?"[16]

16] WILLIAM CULLEN BRYANT. Autograph manuscript poem signed ("W.C. Bryant"), "Not Yet." [N.p.: ca. 1860s]. 2 pages, 9⅜″ x 7¾″.

Written during the summer of 1861 and published in the *New York Ledger* for August 17, 1861, Bryant's patriotic poem is a zealous call to arms against the South:

> And we, who wear thy glorious name,
> Shall we, like cravens, stand apart,
> When those whom thou hast trusted aim
> The death-blow at thy generous heart?
> Forth goes the battle-cry, and lo!
> Hosts rise in harness, shouting, No!

16. Belle Ackison, *The Sunny Side of a Shut-In's Life: A Book of Amusing, Interesting and Helpful Letters* (New York: J. S. Ogilvie, 1902), 54.

Bryant was a strong supporter of the use of military force to preserve the Union. He was critical of the Lincoln administration for not acting forcefully enough, and called for extreme measures against the Confederacy: "the more energetic, the more forceful those measures, the more telling the blow, the more they will applaud."[17]

17] OLIVER WENDELL HOLMES. Autograph manuscript poem fragment signed ("Oliver Wendell Holmes"), "The Flower of Liberty." Boston, January 22, 1864. One page, 6⅞″ by 4⅜″.

In the early days of the Civil War, a Committee Upon a National Hymn was founded to establish a national anthem for the United States. In an announcement dated May 17, 1861, the committee offered a prize of $500 (or a gold medal of equivalent value) to the writer of a song that gave "poetic expression to the emotion which stirs the heart of the nation."[18] The contest received over 1,200 submissions, among them contributions by major authors of the day like Oliver Wendell Holmes, who submitted three poems, including "Union and Liberty" and "The Flower of Liberty." Holmes also had copies of these poems privately printed for the committee.[19]

From the start, the committee's project was met with skepticism. An editorial in *Harper's Weekly* declared: "National hymns are not made to order. They spring from the sudden inspiration of great emotions."[20] (The editorial concludes with a quotation from "The Star-Spangled Banner," written over fifty years earlier and already a popular patriotic song, though it was not made the country's official anthem until 1931.) In August, the committee announced that none of the contributions would be awarded the prize, and shortly thereafter committee member Richard Grant White published a book

17. Quoted in Gilbert H. Muller, *William Cullen Bryant: Author of America* (Albany: State University of New York Press, 2008), 266.
18. Richard Grant White, *National Hymns: How They Are Written and How They Are Not Written; A Lyric and National Study for the Times* (New York: Rudd & Carleton, 1861), 65.
19. Eleanor M. Tilton, *The Parkman Dexter Howe Library, Part IX: Oliver Wendell Holmes* (Gainesville, FL: University of Florida, 1993), 40.
20. "A National Hymn," *Harper's Weekly* 5, no. 231 (June 1, 1861): 338.

about the project entitled *National Hymns: How They Are Written and How They are Not Written.* White published the texts of several of the contest entries, along with an explanation of why each was rejected. In general, he praised the patriotism of the songs, but he was less magnanimous regarding their literary quality: "The sins against good taste in a literary point of view were numberless; many of the songs being in this respect only one monstrous crime in four acts, being four stanzas."[21]

White did not mention Holmes's submission in his book, though he does identify Holmes—along with Longfellow, Poe, and others—as exemplars of American national literature. "The Flower of Liberty" was published in the November 1861 issue of the *Atlantic Monthly*, shortly after the committee had announced the failure of its project. Though it did not win the $500 prize, the poem proved popular enough to be set to music by composer Obadiah Bruen Brown in the year after its publication,[22] and it was the lead poem in an eponymous compilation of patriotic verse edited by Julia A. M. Furbish, published in 1869 as an honorary offering to the veterans of the Civil War.[23] This manuscript fragment, consisting of the poem's final stanza, was written, likely in response to an autograph request, in 1871.

18] WASHINGTON IRVING. Autograph manuscript fragment from *A History of the Life and Voyages of Christopher Columbus.* [N.p., ca. 1826–1828]. One page, 7⅞" x 4½".

Though he was to become a towering figure in American literature, Washington Irving spent much of his career abroad, spending nearly two decades in Europe from 1815 to 1832. While overseas, he wrote some of his best-remembered works, including "Rip Van Winkle" (1819) and "The Legend of Sleepy Hollow" (1820).

21. White, *National Hymns*, 113.
22. Obadiah Bruen Brown, *2 National Songs, The Flower of Liberty [&] Union and Liberty; from the Atlantic Monthly* (Boston: Russell & Patee, 1862). Despite the title, the only copy of the sheet music reported in WorldCat, at the Houghton Library at Harvard University, contains only "The Flower of Liberty."
23. Julia A. M. Furbish, ed., *The Flower of Liberty* (Boston: Benjamin B. Russell, 1869).

Irving was searching for a new literary project in early 1826, when he received a letter from Alexander Hill Everett, who had just been appointed as America's envoy to Spain by John Quincy Adams. Everett offered Irving an honorary position in his legation in Madrid, where he would be given access to Spanish archives, in particular documents relating to Christopher Columbus.[24] (Everett himself had literary interests, having contributed to the *North American Review*, and after his return to Boston in 1829 he became part owner of the journal; his essays on European authors were an important influence on Transcendentalism.)[25]

Irving immersed himself in the Spanish archives in Madrid, and wrote three books based on his research there: *A History of the Life and Voyages of Christopher Columbus*, *A Chronicle of the Conquest of Granada*, and *Voyages and Discoveries of the Companions of Columbus*. His initial intention was to translate his Spanish sources, but the work soon took on both a scholarly and a creative aspect, and he lent his authorial voice to the narrative of his source materials. In an 1827 letter to his nephew, Pierre Munro Irving, he wrote:

> I have been working very hard at the History of Columbus, and have had to re-write many parts that I had thought finished, in consequence of procuring better sources of information, which threw new light on various points. It is a kind of work that will not bear hurrying; many questions have been started connected with it which have been perplexed by tedious controversies, and which must all be looked into. I had no idea of what a complete labyrinth I had entangled myself in when I took hold of the work.[26]

The present manuscript reflects these comments, differing in several major respects to the published version of the text.

Christopher Columbus was an important work in Irving's career, cementing his position as a major American author. Though based on his work overseas, it is a distinctly and deliberately American

---

24. Andrew Burstein, *The Original Knickerbocker: The Life of Washington Irving* (New York: Basic Books, 2007), 191.

25. Tiffany K. Wayne, "Everett, Alexander Hill," *Encyclopedia of Transcendentalism* (New York: Facts On File, 2006), 103.

26. Washington Irving to Pierre Munro Irving, Feb. 22, 1827. In Pierre Munro Irving, *The Life and Letters of Washington Irving* (New York: G. P. Putnam, 1862), 2:257.

work. Irving had faced criticism for spending so much time overseas, and he hoped that the book would silence this criticism by
"fulfill[ing] one of the desiderata of American literature: the creation
of an American hero."[27]

19] HENRY DAVID THOREAU. Autograph manu-
script leaf from *Walden*. [N.p., ca. 1845–1854]. 2 pages,
9¼″ x 7¼″ inlaid in leaf measuring 10¼″ x 8¾″.

In this manuscript leaf from *Walden*, Thoreau discusses the absur-
dity of the conventions by which we have named our natural sur-
roundings. Arising from a discussion (not present in this fragment)
of Flint's Pond, named for a farmer on whose property the pond was
situated, Thoreau mocks the idea that a natural feature should be
named after a person, and the associated concept that any part of
nature could be the property of an individual. Thoreau paints a cari-
cature of Flint as a farmer obsessed with wealth:

> I respect not his labors, his farm where everything has its price; who
> would carry the landscape, who would carry his God to market if he
> could get anything for Him; who goes to market *for* his god as it is;
> on whose farm nothing grows free, whose fields bear no crops, whose
> meadows no flowers, whose trees no fruits, *but dollars; who loves
> not the beauty of his fruits, whose fruits are not ripe for him till they
> are turned to dollars. Give me the poverty that enjoys true wealth.
> Farmers are respectable and interesting to me in proportion as they
> are poor, — poor farmers.[28]

He goes on to describe a model farm, whose crops are "manured
with the hearts and brains of men."[29] Thoreau concludes by stating
that "if the fairest features of the landscape are to be named after
men, let them be the noblest and worthiest men alone." (This final
word is an addition in pencil in the manuscript). This fragment of
Thoreau's most famous work epitomizes the author's approach to
nature as something awe-inspiring and transcendent.

27. John D. Hazlett, "Literary Nationalism and Ambivalence in Washington Irving's *The Life and Voyages of Christopher Columbus*," *American Literature* 55,
no. 4 (December 1983): 562.
28. Henry David Thoreau, *Walden, Or, Life in the Woods* (Boston: Ticknor and
Fields, 1854), 212–13. * Indicates the beginning of this manuscript fragment.
29. Ibid., 213.

20] HENRY WADSWORTH LONGFELLOW. Autograph manuscript poem fragment signed ("Henry W. Longfellow"), "The Building of the Ship" ("Sail On, O Ship Of State!"). [N.p., 1871]. One page, 8⅞″ x 7″.

Though often remembered only for the concluding lines contained in this manuscript fragment, "The Building of the Ship" ranks among Longfellow's best-remembered poems. The extended metaphor on the state as a sailing vessel was written in late 1849, running in one manuscript to nearly eighty pages. The image of the state as a ship was borrowed from ancient sources, appearing in both Plato's *Republic* and Horace's *Odes*. Longfellow's initial draft of the poem was pessimistic, with the vessel smashed on a rock and its builder forgotten. The optimistic and patriotic revised ending, beginning with the famous line "Sail on! Sail on! O Ship of State!" was added to a revised text of the poem completed on November 11, 1849.[30] The revision, which was written the day before an election in which Longfellow cast a vote for the abolitionist Free Soil Party, may reflect the poet's long-standing opposition to slavery.[31]

"The Building of the Ship" was an instant success, and Higginson referred to it as "perhaps the most complete and artistic [poem] which he ever wrote."[32] The poem has been a source of inspiration to leaders in times of crisis. Abraham Lincoln, hearing the poem read in 1862, was brought to tears by its concluding lines.[33] Nearly eighty years later, in January 1941, Franklin Roosevelt sent a quotation from the same passage to Winston Churchill.[34] Churchill incorporated the

30. Hans-Joachim Lang and Fritz Fleischmann, "'All This Beauty, All This Grace': Longfellow's 'The Building of the Ship' and Alexander Slidell Mackenzie's 'Ship,'" *The New England Quarterly* 54, no. 1 (March 1981): 106–7, doi:10.2307/365733.
31. Henry Wadsworth Longfellow Dana, "'Sail On, O Ship of State!' How Longfellow Came to Write These Lines 100 Years Ago," *Colby Library Quarterly* series 2, no. 13 (February 1950): 211–12.
32. Thomas Wentworth Higginson, *Henry Wadsworth Longfellow* (Boston and New York: Houghton, Mifflin and Company, 1902), 200; see also Lang and Fleischmann, "All This Beauty, All This Grace," 104–6.
33. Noah Brooks, "Lincoln's Imagination," *Scribner's Monthly*, August 1879.
34. Dana, "'Sail On, O Ship of State!' How Longfellow Came to Write These Lines 100 Years Ago," 214.

quotation into the conclusion of his "Give Us the Tools" speech broad-cast on February 9, in which he pleaded with America for assistance against the Axis powers.[35] Longfellow's words resound to this day as an example of the powerful role that poetry can play in world affairs.

21⌐ HENRY WADSWORTH LONGFELLOW. Auto-graph manuscript, "The Arrow and the Song," [with] au-tograph letter signed to Mrs. I. S. Wendell. Cambridge, March 15, 1881. 2 pages, 6¾″ x 4⅜″. Letter text published in *The Letters of Henry Wadsworth Longfellow*, ed. An-drew R. Hilen (Cambridge: Belknap Press of Harvard University Press, 1966), vol. 6, p. 698 (letter 4830).

> *I shot an arrow into the air,*
> *It fell to earth, I knew not where . . .*

Another of Longfellow's most famous poems, "The Arrow and the Song" (see plate 2) is a three-stanza poem describing an aim-lessly fired arrow representing the unexpected impact of the poet's words. The poem appeared in Longfellow's collection *The Belfry of Bruges and Other Poems*. Recounting its composition, Longfel-low wrote: "October 16, 1845. Before church, wrote The Arrow and the Song, which came into my mind as I stood with my back to the fire, and glanced on to the paper with arrow's speed. Literally an improvisation."[36] This picture of the poem's composition is compli-cated by the text's similarity to an idea from Goethe's *Sprichwörth-lich*, noted by scholar H. Z. Kip: Longfellow's "improvisation" elabo-rates on Goethe's quatrain, which also uses an aimlessly fired arrow as a metaphor for the spread of a poetic idea.[37]

The present manuscript of the poem was sent to a Mrs. I. S. Wen-

35. Winston Churchill, "Give Us the Tools," *The Churchill Centre*, 2016, http://www.winstonchurchill.org/resources/speeches/1941-1945-war-leader/give-us-the-tools (accessed November 20, 2016).
36. Herbert Cahoon, Thomas V. Lange, and Charles Ryskamp, *American Lit-erary Autographs, from Washington Irving to Henry James* (New York: Dover Publications, 1977), 33.
37. H. Z. Kip, "The Origin of Longfellow's The Arrow and the Song," *Philological Quarterly* 9 (1930): 76–78.

dell of Detroit. Mrs. Wendell had written to Longfellow on March 12 requesting an autograph copy of the poem; nothing else is known about her.[38]

———

"FLATTERING REQUESTS": *PLEASING THE AUTOGRAPH HOUNDS*

22⌉ HENRY WADSWORTH LONGFELLOW. Autograph manuscript fragment signed ("Henry W. Longfellow") of the poem "The Day is Done." [N.p., n.d.]. Partial leaf, approximately 3¾″ x 5½″. Framed with an albumen print of an 1867 photograph of Longfellow by John Adam Whipple.

23⌉ EDGAR ALLAN POE. Autograph letter signed ("Edgar A. Poe") to Oscar T. Keeler. Philadelphia, July 18, 1842. Single leaf, 1 page, 10″ x 7⅞″. With integral address panel, seal remnant, and postmark. Published: John Ward Ostrom, ed.; revised, corrected, and expanded by Burton R. Pollin and Jeffrey A. Savoye. *The Collected Letters of Edgar Allan Poe*, 3rd ed. New York: The Gordian Press, 2008, 1:354–355 (Letter 141b).

> Dr Sir,
> It gives me pleasure to comply with the very flattering request embodied in your letter of June 18th. My absence from this city will, I hope, serve as sufficient apology for the tardiness of this reply.
>> With Respect,
>> Yr ob st.
>>> Edgar A. Poe
> Oscsr T. Keeler Esqre
>> Philadelphia,
>> July 18, 42

38. Henry Wadsworth Longfellow, *The Letters of Henry Wadsworth Longfellow*, ed. Andrew R. Hilen (Cambridge: Belknap Press of Harvard University Press, 1966), v. 6:698.

24⌉ HARRIET BEECHER STOWE. Autograph note signed ("H B Stowe"). [N.p., n.d.]. Partial leaf, approximately 3½″ x 2⅛″.

These relatively undistinguished notes are typical responses to autograph requests. Longfellow provides a quatrain from a well-known portrait, while Stowe's signature comes below a motto: "Trust in the Lord and *do good.*" Poe's letter contains a brief note thanking his correspondent for "the very flattering request" for an autograph. For successful authors of the nineteenth century, producing "album-specimens" of this type for autograph collectors was a regular occurrence, and at times a great nuisance. In an 1857 diary entry, Longfellow stated: "To-day I wrote, sealed, and dictated seventy autographs."[39] The recipients of Longfellow and Stowe's album specimens are unknown, but we have a fair amount of information about Oscar T. Keeler: he was the author of *Keeler's Mississippi Almanac* and served as an agent in Columbus for Philadelphia publications.[40] He was also a noted autograph collector: his collection was auctioned in 1868, and in addition to this letter (sold as lot 754), included the autographs of other major authors, including Longfellow, Emerson, and Lowell.[41]

25⌉ OLIVER WENDELL HOLMES. Manuscript fragment signed ("Oliver Wendell Holmes") from "The Chambered Nautilus." Boston: February 17, 1872. 1 page, 4½″ x 7½″. Framed with a cabinet photograph of Holmes, signed and dated February 22, 1884.

26⌉ OLIVER WENDELL HOLMES. Manuscript fragment signed ("Oliver Wendell Holmes") from "The Chambered Nautilus." Boston: November 30, 1886. 1 page, 4½″ x 7″.

39. A. M. Broadley, *Chats on Autographs.* London: T. Fisher Unwin, 1910, p. 40.
40. "Keeler's Mississippi Almanac," *Godey's Lady's Book* 46, no. 1 (January 1853): 88.
41. *Catalogue of the Entire Collection of Autographs, of Mr. O. T. Keeler, Columbus, Miss.: The Result of Thirty Years Labor in Collecting and the Whole to Be Sold by Auction, at the Clinton Hall Art Galleries & Book Sale Rooms, New York* (New York: Leavitt, Strebeigh & Co., 1868), 18, 33, 43.

"The Chambered Nautilus" was one of Holmes's most successful poems. The poem was first published in the February 1858 issue of the *Atlantic Monthly* as part of an essay in Holmes's "Autocrat of the Breakfast-Table." These two manuscript fragments of the poem's final stanza suggest its popularity: though dated fourteen and twenty-eight years after the poem's first publication, respectively, they are virtually identical, right down to the spacing and indentation of the lines. Both fragments were almost certainly written in response to autograph requests by admirers. There is much to suggest that "The Chambered Nautilus" was Holmes's favorite of his own works, as well: his bookplate featured an image of a nautilus shell.

27⎤ WASHINGTON IRVING, SAMUEL L. CLEMENS, and EDWARD EVERETT HALE. Three autograph notes signed ("Washington Irving", "Mark Twain", "Edward E. Hale") to R. Winchell. Sunnyside [Tarrytown, N.Y.], Sept. 12, 1848; New York, Feb. 12, 1901; [Boston?], Feb. 19, 1907. 1 leaf, 4¾″ x 10⅜″.

[Right panel]

Sunnyside, Sept. 12th 1848

Dear Sir

    In compliance with your request I send you my autograph.

Respectfully
Your ob. Svt.
Washington Irving

Mr. R. Winchell Esq.

[Left panel]

New York, Feb. 12, 1901.

Dear Sir:

    [Consider Mr. Irving's note re-written, here].

Truly Yours,
Mark Twain

Mr. Irving was most cordial in his welcome to younger men – & would have been well pleased to know that a letter of his would be saved so long. Edward E. Hale
Feb. 19, 1907

27] Washington Irving, Samuel L. Clemens, and Edward Everett Hale. Three autograph notes signed to R. Winchell.

This note contains brief inscriptions by three different authors, spanning over half a century. Irving's initial note—a standard response to an autograph request—is fairly unremarkable, but the addition of notes from two other prominent American authors over fifty years later is unique. Moreover, each of the later additions embodies its writer's outlook: Hale takes a formal and obliging tone, while Clemens's addition is humorous and slightly cantankerous (Irving's original note already being fairly impersonal). This single leaf links three generations of authors, illustrating the growth and change in American letters throughout the nineteenth century. Washington Irving was among the earliest authors to attempt to create a truly American literature; Edward Everett Hale, a Unitarian minister closely connected to prominent members of the Transcendentalist movement, found his greatest success from "The Man Without a Country," a powerful allegory of the Civil War; and Mark Twain was the first truly international celebrity to emerge from the world of American literature. More than mere autographs, these three notes show the changing nature of literary success in the nineteenth century.

CHAPTER TWO

The Legacy of the Saturday Club: Boston Authors

———

28⌉ HENRY WADSWORTH LONGFELLOW. Autograph letter signed ("H.W.L.") to Nathaniel Hawthorne. Cambridge, January 30, 1855. 4 pages on a single folded leaf, 6″ x 4″. Not published in Hilen's *The Letters of Henry Wadsworth Longfellow.*

Cambridge, Jan 30
1855

Dear Hawthorne,

You say to me "I shall be happy to be the medium of your English correspondence." But that is not exactly the point. I want to know if it costs you anything: for if it does, you must not think of it, unless you will open a mercantile account with me. If I pay pence and you pay shillings, this new Ocean Penny Postage of mine is a failure. Let me know.

Meanwhile, I try it once more, having some letters ready, and hoping all the while that I am not imposing on your good nature.

Please tell Mr. Bright, that I cannot furnish him with an autograph of Poe, at present, but will try to get one.

Lowell is delivering some delightful Lectures in Boston on English Poets. I think he will be my successor in the College. What do you think of it?

It is a great pity that you do not take more heartily to the English. Why is it?

I wish I could come to England before you leave it. But I do not believe I shall. I have not the courage to move with so many children.

With kind regards to your wife,

Ever Yours,
H. W. L.

The Title page should read thus:

Past and Present.

By

Thomas Carlyle.

Ernst ist das Leben. (German letters)

Schiller.

Boston: Little & Brown

1843

American Editor's Notice.

This book is printed from a private copy, partly in manuscript, sent by the author to his friends in this country, and is published for his benefit. I hope this notice that the profits of the sale of this edition are secured

PLATE 3.
33] Ralph Waldo Emerson. Autograph manuscript of the "American Editor's Notice" and a draft title page for Thomas Carlyle's *Past and Present* (recto).

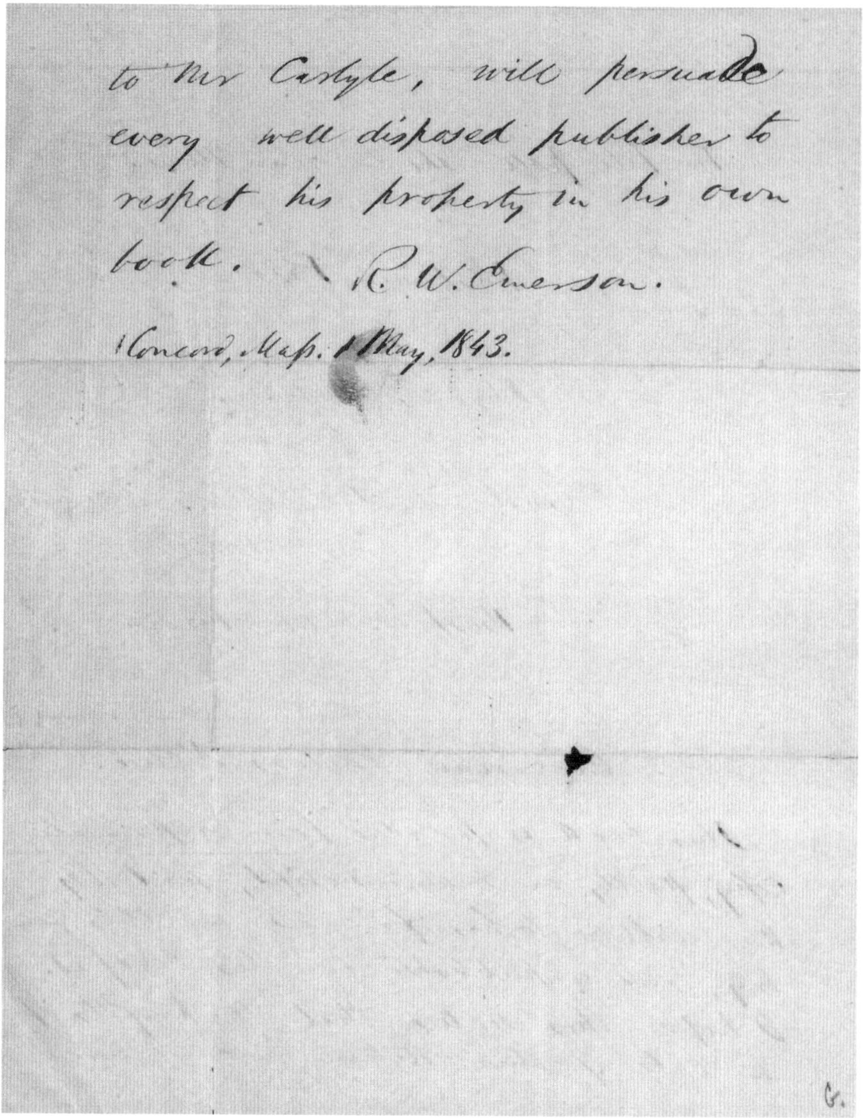

to Mr Carlyle, will persuade every well disposed publisher to respect his property in his own book.

R. W. Emerson.

Concord, Mass. 1 May, 1843.

PLATE 4.
33] Ralph Waldo Emerson. Autograph manuscript of the "American Editor's Notice" and a draft title page for Thomas Carlyle's *Past and Present* (verso).

29] NATHANIEL HAWTHORNE. *Mosses from an Old Manse*. London: Wiley & Putnam, 1846. Two volumes. First edition, first printing in original green cloth. London issue, comprising the American sheets with a cancel title-page bearing the London imprint. Oliver Wendell Holmes's copy: the second volume contains his "Chambered Nautilus" bookplate, and the first contains a later bookplate bearing the same image and an added caption reading "From the library of Oliver Wendell Holmes. The gift of his son Oliver Wendell Holmes."

29] Oliver Wendell Holmes, Jr.'s variant of his father's bookplate, from their copy of Nathaniel Hawthorne's *Mosses from an Old Manse.*

30] HENRY WADSWORTH LONGFELLOW. Autograph letter to Felix Octavius Carr Darley. Cambridge, November 12, 1860. 4 pages on a single folded leaf, 7″ x 4½″. The original signature, and corresponding text from the recto of the leaf, has been clipped and replaced with a separate mounted signature ("Henry W. Longfellow") dated 1880. Not published in Hilen's *The Letters of Henry Wadsworth Longfellow*.

> Cambridge Nov 12
> 1860.
>
> Dear Mr. Darley
> Pardon me for not having written sooner. For the last ten days I have been busy and crowded in many ways.
> But the main business has not been for a moment neglected: I have been twice to Whipple, and should have been again but for the rainy week we have had.
> The report thus far is; body and book successful; face not satisfactory to Gods or men.
> Hawthorne and Emerson have already sat for you, but not with entire success. I told Mr. Whipple you move in haste. He is kind, but slow in the harness. Next time I will put a snapper on the whip.

I expect to see both Hawthorne and Emerson to-day: and will tell them how important it is[. . .] [section missing]

[. . .]says he looks like "a boned pirate." One of his ancestors was a privateersman. Perhaps that accounts for it.

We have had one letter from Tom. He is in London.

[The original signature has been clipped from this letter, and a separate signature ("Henry W. Longfellow. 1880") has been mounted in its place.]

F.O.C. Darley Esq

For much of the nineteenth century Boston was essentially the heart of the American literary scene. Many of the most prominent and successful authors of the time made their homes there, and beginning in 1854 many of them began attending the monthly meetings of The Saturday Club, a gathering of authors, philosophers, and others. Among the attendees of these gatherings were well-known authors like Henry Wadsworth Longfellow, Ralph Waldo Emerson, and James Russell Lowell.[42] These regular meetings soon led to the founding of an important periodical that survives to this day, the *Atlantic Monthly*.

Henry Wadsworth Longfellow was among the most successful American poets of the nineteenth century, and perhaps more than any other author he represented the central position of Boston in American literature of his day. Born in Portland, Maine, Longfellow attended Bowdoin College in the same class as another major author of the nineteenth century: Nathaniel Hawthorne. The two were little acquainted in their youth, and they did not become friends until after the publication of Hawthorne's *Twice-Told Tales* in 1837.[43]

Hawthorne's reputation grew rapidly after the release of *Twice-Told Tales*, as did his friendships with other authors, particularly in New England. Among his friends were Herman Melville and Oliver Wendell Holmes, both of whom lived near Hawthorne in western Massachusetts, and Ralph Waldo Emerson, whose grandfather, William Emerson, built the "Old Manse" in Concord, where Hawthorne lived and wrote many of his stories in the 1840s. A tangible sign of

42. Edward Waldo Emerson, *The Early Years of the Saturday Club, 1855–1870* (Boston and New York: Houghton Mifflin Company, 1918).
43. Manning Hawthorne, "The Friendship between Hawthorne and Longfellow," *The English Journal* 28, no. 3 (March 1939): 221, doi:10.2307/806413.

the friendship between Hawthorne and Holmes is Holmes's copy of *Mosses from an Old Manse*. Both volumes of the work contain Holmes's bookplate with an image of a nautilus, after Holmes's poem "The Chambered Nautilus." (The first volume contains a variant of the bookplate indicating that the book had passed on to Oliver Wendell Holmes, Jr., who sat on the Supreme Court for three decades.)

Hawthorne wrote a campaign biography of Franklin Pierce, who had attended Bowdoin College with both Hawthorne and Longfellow. Shortly after his inauguration in 1853, Pierce appointed Hawthorne to a diplomatic position in Liverpool. There, he offered to serve as a conduit for his American friend's English correspondence, an offer to which this letter, dated January 30, 1855, responds (item 28). Longfellow expresses concern at the potential cost of this arrangement to Hawthorne. In part, this may reflect ongoing concern for Hawthorne's finances: Longfellow had contributed money to Hawthorne's support after he lost his position at the Boston Custom House in 1848. (He needn't have worried for Hawthorne's finances: the consulship at Liverpool was a lucrative one, entitling Hawthorne to a salary as well as a percentage of the income from all American shipping through the city's busy port.)[44]

The importance of Boston in the world of American literature made it the center of the expanding circle of American literary fame. In an 1860 letter to portraitist Felix Octavius Carr Darley, we see Longfellow discussing the growing role of authors as celebrities. He discusses his difficulties having an acceptable portrait taken by "Mr. Whipple," likely the Boston-based photographer John Adams Whipple, co-founder of the studio Whipple and Black. (A daguerreotype of Longfellow taken by Whipple and Black—possibly the portrait referred to in this letter, though no book is visible in the image—is in the collection of the Museum of Modern Art in New York.)[45] Darley, who by 1860 was based on Claymont, Delaware, probably hoped to

44. James R. Mellow, *Nathaniel Hawthorne in His Times* (Boston: Houghton Mifflin, 1980), 415.
45. John Adams Whipple, "Henry Wadsworth Longfellow," Daguerreotype, ca. 1860. Accession no. 590.1953, Museum of Modern Art, https://www.moma.org/collection/works/55423 (accessed October 20, 2016).

paint Longfellow's portrait based on Whipple's photograph. Longfellow's comment that he had plans to see both Hawthorne and Emerson likely refers to a dinner held in honor of Richard Henry Dana the night that the letter was written.[46]

31] RALPH WALDO EMERSON. Autograph letter signed ("R. Waldo Emerson") to Oliver Wendell Holmes. Concord, May 7, 1866. 3 pages, 8″ x 5″. Text unpublished, but summarized in Ralph L. Rusk, ed. *The Letters of Ralph Waldo Emerson*, vol. 5. New York and London: Columbia University Press, 1939, p. 462.

Concord
7 May 1866

My dear Holmes,
   The one feature which is new & attractive in Mr. Pennell's plan is its suggestion of a literary fellowship of three countries, & it is made good for two of them by his gift of brilliant names & I think he has made an excellent beginning in America by his desi[g]n to engage yourself & Lowell in his enterprise. I hope he will succeed in persuading you to join him. For myself I fear I am a dull hand at a magazine, but as the project in its essence seems to require cooperation, I am content to join you, if you decide to enter it. I confess too that my fancy is piqued by the thought of writing in the same journal with Mr. Sainte-Beuve; &, if you think fit, you shall say to Mr. Pennell that if his project goes into effect, I will endeavor to send him a paper.
Always yours,
R. Waldo Emerson

The appeal and fame of Boston authors was not limited to North America. This brief letter from Emerson to Holmes mentions a proposal by an Englishman to establish a magazine that would represent a "literary fellowship of three countries": America, Britain, and France. H. Cholmondeley-Pennell, an English naturalist and author of light verse, contacted a number of authors on both sides of the Atlantic regarding this project. His letter to Emerson does not survive, but it was likely similar to one he sent to Henry Longfellow on December 4, 1865, in which he described his plan:

46. Longfellow, *The Letters of Henry Wadsworth Longfellow*, 4:198 (Letter 1830).

To get, if possible, a majority of the most brilliant writers of the day in England, with a proportion of the more markedly prominent of those of France and America, to unite in supporting by their names and occasional articles a common organ, or as it were an international periodical, for the interchange of thought and literature; and it is believed that if such a combination could be obtained a magazine, to which all thus hitherto attempted would be as dwarfs, must be the result.[47]

A manuscript outline of the project accompanying the letter to Longfellow lays out Pennell's ideas in more detail. His plan was to publish only highly regarded authors, and believed that by doing so he could reach circulation numbers unheard of in the nineteenth century: in a manuscript outline of the project accompanying the letter to Longfellow, he suggests that they could reach 100,000 subscribers.

The proposed magazine was to be published by E. Moxon & Co., with Pennell himself as the editor. Eleanor M. Tilton suggests that the magazine for which Pennell sought support was *The Fortnightly Review*, a London magazine that published its first issue in May 1865.[48] But this identification is likely incorrect: the *Review* was founded prior to Cholmondeley-Pennell's letters seeking support for his own project, was never edited by Pennell, and was not published by Moxon. It appears the project failed to get off the ground, and Pennell does not seem to have ever edited a magazine, though he authored several books in the late nineteenth century, including *Fishing Gossip* and the poetry collection *Puck on Pegasus*.

The "Mr. Saint-Beuve" to whom Emerson refers is Charles Augustin Sainte-Beuve, a French critic, poet, and novelist, most notable for his historical work *Port-Royal*.

47. Henry Cholmondeley-Pennell. Letter to Henry Wadsworth Longfellow, December 4, 1865. Letters to Henry Wadsworth Longfellow, 1761–1888 (bulk). Houghton Library, Harvard University, MS Am 1340.2 (4328).
48. Eleanor M. Tilton, ed. *The Letters of Ralph Waldo Emerson, volume 9: 1860–1869*. New York: Columbia University Press, 1994, p. 227.

CHAPTER THREE
Fortune and Inspiration:
Emerson, Carlyle, & Thoreau

32⌉ THOMAS CARLYLE. *The French Revolution: A History. In Three Volumes.* Boston: Charles C. Little and James Brown, 1838. First American edition; three vols. in two, in original blue-grey embossed cloth. With a gift inscription from Ralph Waldo Emerson to Henry David Thoreau in volume 1 and Thoreau's ownership inscription in volume 2.

33⌉ RALPH WALDO EMERSON. Autograph manuscript signed ("R.W. Emerson"), comprising the "American Editor's Notice" and a draft title page for Thomas Carlyle's *Past and Present.* Concord, Mass., May 1, 1843. 2 pages, 9⅞"x 8".

34⌉ RALPH WALDO EMERSON. Autograph letter signed ("R.W. Emerson") to James Munroe and Company. Concord, Mass., October 10, 1843. 3 pages on two adjoining sheets, 10"x 8".

> Concord, 10 Oct. 1843
>
> Gentlemen,
>
> Mr. Sartain of Phila.ᵃ applied to me lately, on the subject of Carlyle's portrait, thinking I had a better one than the D'Orsay profile. I have that one, & also the full length sketch, a duplicate of the one you send me. Mr. S. wished it for Campbells Magazine, & I suppose is now preparing one of the two for that work. Had you not better buy of him, than make a new engraving? I am content to pay half the cost, if as you propose.

Mr. S.J. May of Lexington told Mr. Lane lately that he had reck-
oned himself a subscriber to the Dial, but that it is never sent him. Is
he on your list?

Our Concord numbers have surely arrived very late & slow.

Will Mr. Munroe have the goodness to furnish me from the books
of his old firm the balances credited & paid in January 1842 & in July
1842 (or in Apr. & October, if those were the dates) to me, on account
of the Carlyle Miscellanies & all vols. & all editions / as I wish to find
Mr. C. an account immediately, & cannot now come at my file of bills
for that year. Please send this information by mail and oblige yours
respectfully,

R.W. Emerson.

Please to hold me accountable for the subscriptions to the Dial of

	Nils P. Ward	
X	Mr. Edmund Hosmer	} Concord
	J.M. Cheney, Esq.	

[Added pencil note in a different hand:]

June 13th 42 note on but 360.58

35] RALPH WALDO EMERSON. *Fortune of the Re-public. Lecture delivered at the Old South Church, March 30, 1878.* Boston: Houghton, Osgood, and Company; Cambridge: The Riverside Press, 1878. Presentation copy inscribed to Thomas Carlyle.

Ralph Waldo Emerson met the Scottish author, philosopher, and
historian Thomas Carlyle on a trip to Scotland in 1833, and the two
began a lifelong correspondence. Emerson also became a de facto
agent for Carlyle in America, promoting his work in literary circles
and arranging for the publication of American editions of his works.
The first of these, James Munroe and Company's 1836 edition of
Sartor Resartus, earned little reward for its author, and Joseph
Slater described it as "an act of benevolent piracy."[49] Emerson took
more care with the arrangement for Carlyle's history of the French
Revolution, taking subscriptions for the title in advance, personally

49. Slater, Joseph, ed., *The Correspondence of Emerson and Carlyle.* New York:
Columbia University Press, 1964, p. 18.

underwriting the finances of the publication, and relinquishing all of his own profits from the book to the author. Writing to Carlyle on November 2, 1837, Emerson writes: " . . . if so good a book can have a tolerable sale, (almost contrary to the nature of a good book, I know,) I shall sustain with glee the new relation of being your banker and attorney."[50] The edition sold quickly, and the income from the publication was a boon to Carlyle, who had been in financial difficulty for some time. Carlyle even claimed in a letter to Emerson on March 18, 1836: "It will be a very brave day when cash actually reaches me, no matter what the number of the coins, whether seven or seven hundred, out of Yankee-land; and strange enough, what is not unlikely, if it be the *first* cash I realize for that piece of work,—Angle-land continuing still *in*solvent to me!"[51]

The present copy of Carlyle's *French Revolution* bears a gift inscription to Emerson's own protégé on the front blank of the first volume: "Henry D. Thoreau from R. Waldo Emerson." The second volume bears Thoreau's ownership signature on the front free endpaper.

Emerson, further hoping to escape the feeling of having been a "benevolent pirate" of Carlyle's work, sought to protect the 1843 American edition of Carlyle's *Past and Present*, issued by Little and Brown, from piracy. In a letter to Carlyle on April 29, 1843, Emerson explains the growing financial difficulty of publishing in America:

> You must know that the cheap press has, within a few months, made a total change in our book markets. Every English book of any name or credit is instantly converted into a newspaper or coarse pamphlet, & hawked by a hundred boys in the streets of all our cities for 25, 18, or 12 cents . . . One prints Bulwer's novel yesterday, for 25 cents; and already in twenty four hours, another has a coarser edition of it for 18 cents, in all thoroughfares.[52]

Emerson then lays out his plan to prevent this theft of Carlyle's work, explaining that he had contacted "the great Reprinters, namely to Park Benjamin, & to the Harpers, of New York" to ask that they refrain from reprinting the work and thereby undercutting the publication's

50. Ibid., p. 170.
51. Ibid., p. 180.
52. Ibid., p. 342.

sales.[53] In addition, in a manuscript piece dated May 1 (plates 3-4), Emerson provides a draft title page for the book, as well as a notice published as a preface to the American edition: "This book is printed from a private copy in manuscript, sent by the author to his friends in this country, and is published for his benefit. I hope this notice that the profits of the sale of this edition are secured to Mr. Carlyle, will persuade every well disposed publisher to respect his property in his own book." Unfortunately, the preface failed to dissuade the book pirates, as Emerson explained in a letter to Carlyle on October 30:

> For a few weeks I believed that the letters I had written to the principal New York & Phil[a] booksellers, and *the preface* had succeeded in repelling the pirates. But in the fourth or fifth week appeared a mean edition in N. York published by one Collyer (an unknown person & supposed to be a masque of some other bookseller) sold for 12½ cents and of this wretched copy several thousand were sold, whilst our 75 cent edition went off slower.[54]

Emerson's unsuccessful attempts to preempt the piracy of Carlyle's work illustrate the impact that increased industrialization of the printing process was having on the finances of authors and their publishers. It also shows the growing size of the literate public: if Emerson's report that several thousand copies of the pirated edition sold is accurate, then the audience for works like Carlyle's was sizeable.

As well as looking out for his financial interests, Emerson took some care in shaping Carlyle's public image. In a letter to his publisher, James Munroe, on October 10, 1843, Emerson discusses a new portrait of Carlyle being engraved by John Sartain for *Campbell's Foreign Semi-Monthly Magazine*. Carlyle had sent Emerson a sketch of himself by the Parisian artist Alfred d'Orsay in April 1840, and Emerson had forwarded this sketch to Sartain for engraving. As ever, Emerson takes on financial responsibility for the American presentation of his Scottish hero, offering to share the cost of using the new engraving with Munroe. Emerson goes on to discuss Carlyle's finances, requesting an accounting of income from Carlyle's books published by Munroe so he can set up an account for him.

53. Ibid., p. 343.
54. Ibid., p. 346.

To
Master George W. Sewall,
In consideration of his love of Animated Nature,
The following Poem
Is humbly inscribed
by the Author

The Bluebirds

In the midst of the Poplar that stand by our door
We planted a blue-bird box,
And we hoped before the summer was o'er
A transient pair to coax.

One warm summer's day the blue bird came
And lighted on our tree,
But at first the wanderers were not so tame
But they were afraid of me.

They seemed to come from the distant South,
Just o'er the Walden wood,
And skimmed it along with open mouth
Close by where the bellows stood

Warbling they swept round the distant cliff,
And they warbled it over the lea,
And now o'er the blacksmith's shop in a jiff
Did they come warbling to me

+ a vane of that shape on our
woodshed

36] Henry David Thoreau. Autograph manuscript poem, "The Bluebirds," page 1 of 2.

Emerson's friendship with Carlyle lasted decades, as evidenced by a copy of Emerson's 1878 lecture *Fortune of the Republic* inscribed: "Thomas Carlyle, with entire affection of R.W.E." Thomas Wentworth Higginson, an American visiting Carlyle at the time, recorded his thoughts on this essay, representing the author's brogue phonetically: "I've just noo been reading it; the dear Emerson, he thinks the whole warrld's like himself; and if he can just get a million people together and let them all vote, they'll be sure to vote right and all will go vara weel."[55]

36⌉ HENRY DAVID THOREAU. Autograph manuscript poem, "The Bluebirds." [Concord, Mass., 1839]. 2 pages, 10″ x 8″. Inscribed to George Sewall.

37⌉ [HENRY DAVID THOREAU]. Prudence Ward. Autograph manuscript of Henry David Thoreau's poem "Sympathy." [Concord, Mass.], June 24, 1839. 3 pages, 9¾″ x 7⅞″. "Copied by P.W. from H.D.T.'s lines."

38⌉ RALPH WALDO EMERSON. *The Method of Nature. An Oration, Delivered Before the Society of the Adelphi, in Waterville College, in Maine, August 11, 1841.* Boston: Samuel G. Simpkins, 1841. First edition, in original wrappers. Presentation copy inscribed by Emerson to Henry David Thoreau.

39⌉ HENRY DAVID THOREAU. Autograph manuscript poem, "Inspiration." [N.p., 1841 or later]. 4 pages, 10″ x 8¼″.

40⌉ RALPH WALDO EMERSON. Autograph letter signed ("R.W. Emerson") to Henry David Thoreau. Con-

55. Ibid., p. 60.

cord, Massachusetts, September 8, 1843. 3 pages, 9⅞″ x 8¾″. With integral address leaf in Emerson's hand. Published: Eleanor M. Tilton, ed. *The Letters of Ralph Waldo Emerson, volume VII: 1807-1844*. New York: Columbia University Press, 1990, p. 557–560.

Concord September 8 1843

Dear Henry,

We were all surprised to hear one day lately from G. Waldo that you were forsaking the deep quiet of the Clove for the limbo of the false booksellers, and were soon relieved by hearing that you were safe again in the cottage at S.I. I could heartily wish that this country which seems all opportunity, did actually offer more distinct & just rewards of labor to that unhappy class of men who have more reason & conscience than strength of back & of arm, but the experience of a few cases that I have lately seen looks I confess more like crowded England & indifferent Germany, than like rich & roomy nature. But the few cases are deceptive, and though Homer should starve in the highway, Homer will know & proclaim that bounteous Nature has bread for all her boys. Tomorrow our arms will be stronger, tomorrow the wall before which we sat, will open of itself & show the new way. Ellery Channing works & writes as usual of his cottage to which Captain Moore has added a neat slat fence & gate. His wife as yet has no more than five scholars, but will have more presently. Hawthorn [*sic*] has returned from a visit to the seashore in good spirits. Elizabeth Hoar is still absent since Evarts's marriage. You will have heard of our 'Wyman Trial' & the stir it made in the village. But the Cliff & Walden, which know something of the railroad, knew nothing of that: not a leaf nodded, not a pebble fell: why should I speak of it to you now the humanity of the town suffers with the poor Irish who receives but 60 or even 50 cents for working from dark till dark, with a strain & a following up that reminds one of negro driving. Peter Hutchinson told me he had never seen men perform so much: he should never think it hard again if an employer should keep him at work till after sundown. But what can be done for their relief as long as new applicants for the same labor are coming in every day. These of course reduce the wages to the sum that will suffice a bachelor to live, & must drive out the men with families. The work goes on very fast. The mole which crosses the land of Jonas Potter & Mr. Stow from Ephraim Wheelers highland to the depot, is eighteen ft. high & goes on two rods every day. A few days ago a new contract was completed from the terminus

of the old contract to Fitchburg—the whole to be built before Oct 1844. So that you see our fate is sealed. I have not yet advertised my house for sale, nor engaged by passage to Berkshire: have even suffered George Bradford to plan a residence with me next spring: and at this very day am talking with Mr Britton at building a cottage in my triangle for Mrs Brown: but I can easily foresee that some inconveniences may arise from the road when open, that shall drive me from my rest. I mean to send the "Winters Walk" to the printer tomorrow for the Dial. I had some hesitation about it, notwithstanding its faithful observation & its fine sketches of the pickerel fisher & of the woodchopper, on account of mannerism, an old charge of mine,—as if by attention one could get the trick of the rhetoric, e.g. to call a cold place sultry, a solitude public, a wilderness domestic (a favourite word), & to in the wood, to impress over cities, whilst the woods again are dignified by comparing them to cities, armies, &c. By pretty free omission, however, I have removed my principal objections. I ought to say that Ellery Channing admired the piece loudly & long & only stipulated for the omission of Douglas & one copy of verses on the Smoke. — For the rest, we go on with the month of the Poet & Painter and with extracts from the Jamaica Voyage. And Lane has sent me a Day with the Shakers: poetry have I very little. Have you no Greek translations ready for me? I beg you to tell my brother Wm. that the Review of Channings Poems in the Democratic Review has been interpolated with sentences & extracts to make it long by the Editor & I acknowledge as far as I remember little beyond the first page. And now that I have departed so far from my indolence as to write this long letter I have yet to add to mine the affectionate greetings of my wife & my mother. Yours
R.W. Emerson

41] HENRY DAVID THOREAU. Autograph manuscript fragment from "Chesuncook." [N.p., ca. 1858]. 2 pages, 9¾″ x 7½″. Docketed on the verso by James Russell Lowell.

Perhaps no literary friendship of the nineteenth century is as famous as that between Ralph Waldo Emerson and Henry David Thoreau. The two met in 1837, shortly after Thoreau graduated from Harvard, and Emerson immediately became a mentor to the younger author, encouraging him to write and advocating for him with publishers.

From 1838–1841, Henry Thoreau and his brother John ran a school, the Concord Academy. Among their students was a young Louisa May Alcott, as well as one of her cousins, a boy named Edmund Sewall, then eleven years old.[56] Thoreau was struck by Sewall's spirit, and wrote for him the poem "Sympathy," which begins: "Lately, alas! I knew a gentle boy, / Whose features all were cast in Virtue's mold, / As one she had designed for Beauty's toy, / But after manned him for her own stronghold." Emerson praised the poem in his journal: "The purest strain, and the loftiest, I think, that has yet pealed from this unpoetic American forest."[57] The present manuscript of the poem is written in the hand of Prudence Ward, Sewell's aunt and a boarder in the Thoreau home.

When Edmund's younger brother George complained that he had no poem of his own, Thoreau wrote out his poem "The Bluebirds," beneath the inscription: "To Master George W. Sewall, In consideration of his love of animated Nature, the following Poem is humbly inscribed by the Author." Lance Newman calls this poem "deceptively simple," being both a pleasant description of a breeding pair of birds that set up a nest in a birdhouse and a subtle expression of the ecstatic experience of nature for which Thoreau would become famous.[58] This manuscript of the poem contains only twelve of the complete poem's twenty stanzas. However, one stanza does not appear in either the version he wrote in his journal or in the published text: "But they knew all the while 'twas a house to let / And they knew they wanted to hire, / But they took no pains the house to get, / Nor yet would they retire."

During the same period that they were operating the Concord Academy, Henry and John Thoreau undertook the journey that formed the basis of the book *A Week on the Concord and Merrimack Rivers*. This was a formative time for Thoreau, underscored by John's untimely death from tetanus in 1843. *A Week* became a

56. For more on Edmund Sewall and the Thoreaus' school, see Clayton Hoagland, "The Diary of Thoreau's 'Gentle Boy.'" *The New England Quarterly* 28.4 (1955), p. 473–489.
57. Quoted in Hoagland, p. 473.
58. Lance Newman, "'Patron of the World': Henry Thoreau as Wordsworthian Poet." In *Henry David Thoreau.* Ed. Harold Bloom. Bloom's Modern Critical Views. New York: Infobase Publishing, 2007, p. 115.

memorial for his brother, and the relationship between the Thoreau brothers was an essential part of Henry's development as an author and thinker.

In 1841, Thoreau's time at the Concord Academy ended, and Emerson invited him in to his home, where he stayed until 1843. Emerson gave books to his protégé, among them the above copy (item 32) of Carlyle's *French Revolution* and the 1841 publication of *The Method of Nature*, a lecture originally delivered at Waterville College in 1841, shortly after Thoreau joined his mentor's household. This essay, which discusses nature as "a work of ecstasy," was undoubtedly an influence on the young Thoreau. Emerson describes the effect of this ecstasy:

> That well-known voice speaks in all languages, governs all men, and none ever caught a glimpse of its form. If the man will exactly obey it, it will adopt him, so that he shall not any longer separate it from himself in his thought, he shall seem to be it, he shall be it. If he listen with insatiable ears, richer and greater wisdom is taught him, the sound swells to a ravishing music, he is borne away as with a flood, he becomes careless of his food and of his house, he is the fool of ideas, and leads a heavenly life. (p. 18–19)

Emerson inscribed this copy of *The Method of Nature* with a clear, Transcendentalist simplicity: "Henry D. Thoreau from R.W.E."

We can see the influence of Emerson's conception of ecstasy in Thoreau's poem "Inspiration." This poem was written the same year as Emerson's Waterville address, while Thoreau was resident at Emerson's home. Describing the ineffable experience of epiphany, Thoreau writes: "I hearing get who had but ears, / And sight, who had but eyes before, / I moments live who lived but years, / And truth discern who knew but learning's lore." The present manuscript (plate 5) shows an earlier draft of these famous lines, the last of which here reads "and knowledge have who knew but learning's lore." A correction in Thoreau's hand alters the line to the wording of the published version. Emerson read from "Inspiration" in his eulogy of Thoreau in 1862, devoting more of the oration to this poem than any of Thoreau's other works. The mystical outlook on display in "Inspiration" may have been shaped by Thoreau's exposure to Emerson's library, which included scarce works of Indian philosophy.[59]

In 1843, Thoreau traveled to Staten Island to stay at the home of Emerson's brother William and serve as a tutor to his eldest son. The two maintained a correspondence during his absence in which they discussed news of Concord and New York as well as the editing of the Transcendentalist journal *The Dial*, edited by Margaret Fuller and featuring frequent contributions by Emerson, Thoreau, and others. Thoreau took advantage of his proximity to Manhattan to meet a number of literary figures there, including Horace Greeley and Henry James.[60] He also met with publishers, in hopes of finding employment: in a letter to his mother on August 29, he wrote: "I have tried sundry methods of earning money in the city, of late, but without success: have rambled into every bookseller's or publisher's house, and discussed their affairs with them. Some propose to me to do what an honest man cannot."[61]

Emerson heard of Thoreau's unsuccessful attempts at finding paying work in publishing, and wrote to him on September 8, calling Manhattan "the limbo of the false booksellers" and speaking expansively with words of encouragement for Thoreau and all those hoping to make a living in letters:

> I could heartily wish that this country which seems all opportunity, did actually offer more distinct & just rewards of labor to that unhappy class of men who have more reason & conscience than strength of back & of arm, but the experience of a few cases that I have lately seen looks I confess more like crowded England & indigent Germany, than like rich & roomy Nature. But the few cases are deceptive, and though Homer should starve in the highway, Homer will know and proclaim that bounteous Nature has bread for all her boys. Tomorrow our arms will be stronger, tomorrow the wall before which we sat, will open of itself & show the new way.

59. Walter Harding, *The Days of Henry Thoreau: A Biography*, Princeton Paperback edition (Princeton: Princeton University Press, 1992), 129–30.
60. See F. B. Sanborn, "The Emerson-Thoreau Correspondence: The Dial Period." *The Atlantic Monthly*, May 1892. *The Thoreau Reader*. The Thoreau Society, Aug. 9, 2009. Online. < http://thoreau.eserver.org/letters.html > (accessed Feb. 21, 2016).
61. Henry David Thoreau. *Familiar Letters of Henry David Thoreau*. Ed. F. B. Sanborn. Boston and New York: Houghton, Mifflin, 1894, p. 125.

He goes on to give an extended update on recent developments among their mutual friends and colleagues, mentioning the likes of William Ellery Channing, Nathaniel Hawthorne, Elizabeth Hoar (who assisted in the collection of Thoreau's writings after his death), and George Partridge Bradford. He closes the letter with a critical discussion of Thoreau's essay "A Winter Walk," which he was then editing for *The Dial*, making it clear that he found Thoreau's rhetorical use of paradox grating. "By pretty free omissions," he writes, "I have removed my principal objections." Privately, Emerson disliked this piece, writing in a journal that reading it made him "nervous & wretched,"[62] and thus this letter hints at the growing rift between the two authors.

The early strains in the friendship between Emerson and Thoreau were literary and philosophical: having in many respects idealized one another, neither could quite live up to the other's hopes. Their estrangement became more complete in the late 1840s, in part due to the commercial failure of Thoreau's first book, *A Week on the Concord and Merrimack Rivers*. At Emerson's urging, Thoreau had financed the book himself, and its disappointing sales left him several hundred dollars in debt. Thoreau also complained in his journal that Emerson had failed to provide him with much-needed criticism: instead of giving him an honest account of the book's shortcomings, he provided only positive comments. "While my friend was my friend," Thoreau privately wrote, "he flattered me, and I never heard the truth from him, but when he became my enemy he shot it to me on a poisoned arrow."[63] In light of Emerson's frank critique of Thoreau's prose in "Winter's Walk," this comment is surprising. Jealousy may also have played a role in their estrangement: Sattelmeyer presents compelling evidence that Thoreau, who stayed at Emerson's home as a substitute *paterfamilias* while the elder author was traveling in Europe in 1847–1848, may have been in love with Emerson's wife Lidian.[64] By the early 1850s, Emerson and Thoreau had largely parted ways.

62. Quoted in Robert Sattelmeyer, "'When He Became My Enemy': Emerson and Thoreau, 1848–49." *The New England Quarterly* 62.2 (1989), p. 193.
63. Quoted in Sattelmeyer, p. 190.
64. Ibid., p. 196–203.

Though *A Week* had been a commercial failure, Thoreau was increasingly in demand as a naturalist writer, especially after the 1854 publication of *Walden; or, Life in the Woods.* In 1857, James Russell Lowell asked Thoreau to contribute to the *Atlantic Monthly.* Thoreau and Lowell had attended Harvard together, but they had never been friends, and "Lowell thought Thoreau a self-advertising, romantic egotist"—but still considered him an original enough writer to seek contributions from him for the *Atlantic.*[65] In January 1858 Thoreau submitted the essay "Chesuncook," later to become part of his book *The Maine Woods.* Lowell accepted the piece, but cut out one sentence, a statement, tinged with pantheism, about a pine tree: "It is as immortal as I am, and perchance will go to as high a heaven, there to tower above me still."[66] Lowell had likely cut the sentence for fear of a reaction against its pagan overtones. Thoreau indicated that he wanted the sentence retained, but the text was published with the line still deleted. Thoreau wrote an angry letter to Lowell, declaring: "I am not willing to be associated in any way, unnecessarily, with parties who will confess themselves so bigoted and timid as this implies. I could excuse a man who was afraid of an uplifted fist, but if one habitually manifests fear at the utterance of a sincere thought, I must think that his life is a kind of nightmare continued in broad daylight."[67] The offending sentence is not part of the present manuscript leaf from "Chesuncook," but the text's description of "the universal spiring upward of the forest evergreens" hints at the pine forest as a wild cathedral, and one could certainly imagine its discussion of a paradox in the traditional contrast between the "civilized" city and the "savage" wilderness as being just as controversial as the mystical view of the pine tree.

Thoreau died of tuberculosis on May 6, 1862, and Emerson delivered a long eulogy for him at his memorial service on May 9. The oration, made famous by its publication in the *Atlantic Monthly* that

---

65. Ellery Sedgwick, *A History of the Atlantic Monthly, 1857-1909: Yankee Humanism at High Tide and Ebb.* Amherst: University of Massachusetts Press, 1994, p. 59.
66. Ibid., p. 60.
67. Ibid.

August, shows the strain that had developed between the two authors since their first meeting. Alan D. Hodder writes that the eulogy "appears to have done more to dampen the reading public's esteem than to heighten it . . . Emerson praised Thoreau's gifts, while at the same time noting his obvious eccentricities. To readers expecting a more thoroughgoing apotheosis, Emerson's address seemed wan and thin spirited, as if to damn by faint praise."[68] Even more damaging was a savage posthumous critique of Thoreau's work published by James Russell Lowell in the *North American Review* in 1865. By the late nineteenth century, Thoreau's public image was that of "a reserved, stoical, and unsympathetic person."[69]

68. Alan D. Hodder, *Thoreau's Ecstatic Witness.* New Haven: Yale University Press, 2001, p. 7.
69. F. B. Sanborn, "The Emerson-Thoreau Correspondence: The Dial Period."

Friendship, Advice, and Influence

———

42] EDGAR ALLAN POE. Autograph letter signed ("Edgar A. Poe") to Washington Irving. Philadelphia, October 12, 1839. Single folded leaf, 2 pages, 9¾″ x 7¾″. With integral address panel, seal remnant, and postmark. Docket mark by Irving dated November 6. Published: Ostrom, Pollin, & Savoye, eds., *The Collected Letters of Edgar Allan Poe*, I:198–201 (Letter 83a).

Philadelphia
Octo. 12. 1839.

Dear Sir,

      I duly received your kind letter, and entirely acquiesce in what you say—that it would be improper to force an opportunity of speaking of a detached Tale. I should be grieved, however, if you have supposed that I could make such [a] demand; my request you have fully promised to grant in saying that you will bear me in mind, and "take the first <u>unforced</u> opportunity" of expressing your opinion".

    I take the liberty of sending you the Octo: No: of the Gents' Magazine, containing the Tale "William Wilson". This is the tale of which I spoke in my former letter, and which is based upon a brief article of your own in the first "Gift"—that for 1836. Your article is called "An Unwritten Drama of Lord Byron". I have hoped that, having thus a right of ownership in my "William Wilson", you will be induced to read it—and I also hope that, reading it, you will find in it something to appro[v]e. This brings me to another request, which I hardly know how to urge, and for urging which I am greatly afraid you will think me importunate. I trust, however, you will make allowance for the circumstances in which I am placed, for the difficulties I have to overcome, and for the anxiety which I feel.

    Mess: Lea & Blanchard are about publishing a collection of my Tales, in 2 vols, to be issued early next month. As these Tales, in their course of original publication from time to time, have received many high praises from gentlemen whose opinions are of weight; and as these encomiums have already been published in the papers of the day, (being comprised in notices of the Southern Lit: Messenger and other Magazines) Mess. L & B. think there would be nothing objectionable in their reprinting them, in the ordinary form of an advertisement appended to the various books which they may issue before mine. I do not speak altogether of editorial opinions, but of the personal opinions of some of our principal literary men, which have found their way into the papers Among others, I may mention Mr Paulding, Mr Kennedy & Mr Willis. Now, if, to the very high encomiums which have been lavished upon some of my tales by these & others, I could be permitted to add even a word or two from yourself, in relation to the tale of "William Wilson" (which I consider my best effort) my fortune would be made. I do not say this unadvisedly — for I am deliberately convinced that your good opinion, thus permitted to be expressed, would ensure me that public attention which would carry me on to fortune hereafter, by ensuring me fame at once.

I feel, however, that I am, in regard to yourself an utter stranger — and that I have no claim whatever upon your good offices. Yet I could not feel that I had done all which could be justly done, towards ensuring success, until I had made this request of you. I have a strong hope that you will be inclined to grant it, for you will reflect that what will be an act of little moment in respect to yourself — will be life itself to me.

My request now, therefore, is that, if you approve of "William Wilson", you will express so much in your own terms ∧ in a letter to myself and permit Mess L & B. to publish it, as I mentioned.

Submitting all to your kindness

I am

With highest respect

Edgar A Poe

Washington Irving Esqr

In late 1839, Edgar Allan Poe was preparing for the publication of his first collection of fiction, *Tales of the Grotesque and Arabesque*. Poe and his publishers, Lea & Blanchard, assembled an advertising section containing praise for Poe's stories. Poe sent letters to a number of notable literary figures requesting their opinions to be added to this selection of blurbs. He sent Washington Irving a note along with the September 1839 issue of *Burton's Gentleman's Magazine*, containing "The Fall of the House of Usher," and received positive comments from the author. On October 12, he wrote again to Irving, this time sending the October issue of *Burton's* with the tale "William

Wilson." His cover letter (plates 6-7) explicitly asks for comments for the advertising section, flattering Irving that if he provided any comment whatsoever "my fortune would be made." Irving obliged, sending Poe a brief, positive review of "William Wilson" which appears, alongside comments by John Neal, N. P. Willis, and others, in a section of "Advertisements" in the second volume of *Tales of the Grotesque and Arabesque*: "I have read your little tale of 'William Wilson' with much pleasure. It is managed in a highly picturesque style, and the singular and mysterious interest is well sustained throughout. I repeat what I have said in regard to a previous production, which you did me the favor to send me, that I cannot but think a series of articles of like style and merit would be extremely well received by the public."[70] Irving added a personal note to Poe, containing advice concerning the style of the two stories. This letter shows Poe, at a critical early juncture in his career, seeking the guidance of an established author—one whose work had no doubt been an influence on the younger writer.

43] JAMES RUSSELL LOWELL. Autograph letter signed ("J.R. Lowell") to A. M. Ide, Jr. Cambridge, June 13, 1843. 1 page, 10½″ x 8″. With integral address panel and seal remnant. Published: Kent P. Ljungquist, "'Fellowship with Other Poets': Longfellow, Lowell, and Poe Correspond with A. M. Ide, Jr.," *Resources for American Literary Study* 28 (2002): 31.

Cambridge June 13, 1843.

My dear Sir,

I thank you for that confidence which led you to send me the firstfruits of your muse. It is wholly impossible to judge from many specimens, even, of youthful poetry, (much more so from one), what may be the promise of the writer. I can trace in yours, I think, a vein of natural sentiment, which may be worked to advantage. But you must not write till you have read. You cannot measure yourself till you

---

70. George E. Woodberry, *The Life of Edgar Allan Poe, Personal and Literary, with His Chief Correspondence with Men of Letters*, vol. 1 (Boston: Houghton Mifflin Co., 1909), 216–17.

know what others have done. Study the great poets—they will give you command of language &, what is better, command of self. Read Shakespeare, Spencer, Milton, Wordsworth, Burns, Coleridge, Byron, Keats & Shelley—they will tell you better than I whether you are a poet or not.

You have probably heard by this time of the failure of the "Pioneer."

With all good wishes & hopes for you, I remain

Your friend

J.R. Lowell.

44⌉ HENRY WADSWORTH LONGFELLOW. Autograph letter signed ("Henry W. Longfellow") to A. M. Ide, Jr. Cambridge, June 5, 1843. 2 leaves, 4 pages; 8⅞″ x 7½″. With integral address panel, seal remnant, and postmark. Published: Ljungquist, "Fellowship with Other Poets," 32–33.

Cambridge June 5 1843.

My dear Sir,

I have had the pleasure of receiving your favor of May 29. and shall answer it in the same spirit of frankness in which it is written. I am indeed very glad you have written to me; for having gone over the ground you are now going over, in literary hopes, projects and aspirations, it may be in my power to give you a useful hint or two. Nor will you take this amiss; for I am just twice your age, and can without vanity therefore offer you the light of my experience.

———

In the first place, then, a word as to your position. Were I a farmer, as you are, and had at the same time the gift of song, as you have, I would cling to my position in the world with pride and gratitude. I have great reverence for labor. It gives health of body and health of mind. Hold fast to your inheritance, therefore; be both a farmer and a poet; and give us in your song, the scent of the wild-flowers, and the new-turned soil, and the roar of the forest. Of city poets there are enough; - let us have one good, rigorous, athletic bard with thick shoes and a brown hand. That is what I should aim at being, were I in your place.

———

As to Fame, I have but one word to say. Do not seek for it. It comes — sooner or later — it comes because <u>deserved</u>, not because <u>it is sought after</u>. Write your best, and let your reputation take care of itself. This I have discussed somewhat at length in a book called "<u>Hyperion</u>", and which, if you do not own it, I should be happy to send you, if you care, for my opinion on that matter of <u>literary fame</u>, and if you will tell me how I can send the volumes.

—

As to publishing in Magazines — if I did it at all — I should do it anonymously for the present. You will see the advantage of this hereafter. The few lines you send me show taste and delicacy of feeling; but are not precisely what I want you to write. Indeed it is difficult to say what a man should write; save that <u>it should be himself</u>, and savor of his position and calling.

Have you read Carlyle's Writings? If not, pray read them; — particularly his "Miscellanies", and "Heroes & Hero-Worship." They will cheer and invigorate you; and throw much light on your path.

I have written in great haste; and have not said one tenth part of what I wish to say to you. Pray write me as often and as freely as you feel inclined; and be sure of simplicity in your literary and other undertakings; and when you next visit Boston do not fail to come and see me.   Yours very truly

Henry W. Longfellow.

45⌉ HENRY WADSWORTH LONGFELLOW. Autograph letter signed ("Henry W. Longfellow") to A. M. Ide, Jr. Cambridge, July 4, 1843. 2 leaves, 4 pages; 8⅞″ x 7¼″. Published: Ljungquist, "Fellowship with Other Poets," 34.

Cambridge. July 4 1843

My dear Sir,

You will find ᵐᵉ at best a very poor, and negligent correspondent. I have so many occupations — so many letters to write — so many little things, that steal my time away, that everybody complains of me as a most negligent letter-writer. You must not therefore be surprised if sometimes your letters remain long unanswered, or do not get answered at all.

I was very sorry I did not see you on the 17ᵗʰ. But, as you say, that was not a time to look after anyone. The crowd, the heat, the engagements of each — prevented any possibility of meeting, unless by mere chance. I did not go to Bunker Hill, but passed the day very quietly with some friends in Boston.

You have embarrassed me a little about sending you Hyperion, by not telling me to what address I shall send it. You say <u>leave it somewhere</u>. That is <u>nowhere</u>. I have therefore concluded to <u>send it to the care of B. Cranston & Co Providence</u>, where you will find it when you next go to town, or may send for it at your leisure.

I should like to see in print that last poem of yours. If Willis published it — send it me. I liked it much — that is to say the one stanza you sent. It is far, far better than the others; and is in the vein I want you to labor in. I am glad to say, also, by your letters, that you do not despise your position in the world. Labor alone is honorable, and will inherit the earth and the sky.

As to College Education, I do not think it necessary to eminence, though very likely to contribute alteration. You can certainly attain to excellence without it. Read the English Classics. Read Homer in Chapman's Translation which you can get from Professor Elton of Brown University, an excellent man, whom you ought to know. — Read also Dante, in Cary's Translation for want of a better. Homer and Dante! These are great names! Writers who will nourish your soul. Let Bulwer and the Magazines go for the present. What you want is, neither to weaken your mind by ∧ reading effeminate productions, nor to overload it with too much learning, but to develop and strengthen it with sufficient and convenient food, such as the works of the great masters afford.

Yours very truly
Henry W. Longfellow

46⟧ EDGAR ALLAN POE. Autograph letter signed ("Edgar A. Poe") to A. M. Ide. Jr. Philadelphia, October 19, 1843. Single leaf, 2 pages, 9⅞″ x 7⅞″. With integral address panel, seal remnant, and postmark. Published: Ljungquist, "Fellowship with Other Poets," 35–39; Ostrom, Pollin, & Savoye, eds., *The Collected Letters of Edgar Allan Poe*, I:410–412 (Letter 163d).

Philadelphia, Octo. 19. 1843.

My Dear Sir,

Upon returning to town after a short absence I find your letter of the 1st. and regret that you should have considered it necessary to apologize for addressing me. It will give me true pleasure to hear from you at all times, and I hope you will believe me in earnest when I say so. You ask me for my hand in friendship. I give it with the deepest sincerity. Had I met the few lines you send me, in any journal in the country, I should at once have felt myself the friend of their author— as I am unfeignedly of every man of genius. You well know that I am not given to flattery.

I would say to you, without hesitation, aspire. A literary reputation, it is true, is seldom worth much when attained—for by this time the appetite for applause is sated—but in the struggle for its attainment is the true recompense. You are young, enthusiastic, and possess high talents. You will not fail of success. Be bold—read much—write much—publish little—keep aloof from the little wits, and fear nothing.

I hope you will write me frequently and freely, and regard me as your friend, and consider me bound to further your literary interests as far as lies in my power. That power, at present, is little. By and bye it may be more. In the meantime I may treat you as frankly as you have treated myself, and call upon you for aid in a good cause—in a very bold and comprehensive enterprise.—to aid in which I am already privately marshaling the true talent and chivalry of the land—I mean an enterprise which shall elevate this true talent upon the throne of the great usurper called Humbug. At present, the Bobby Buttons rule the world of American Letters—but we must change all that—and if no one else will stir effectively in the task, I must and will.

I write these few words in extreme haste, and merely to say that I feel honored by your demand. At some future day I will communicate with you more fully.

Believe me

Yours most sincerely

A.M.Ide Jr   Edgar A Poe

47⌐ EDGAR ALLAN POE. Autograph letter signed ("Edgar A. Poe") to A. M. Ide. Jr. [New York]: January 25, 1845. Single leaf, 2 pages, 9¾″ x 7⅞″. With integral address panel, seal remnant, and postmark. Published: Ljungquist, "Fellowship with Other Poets," 40–43; Ostrom, Pollin, & Savoye, eds., *The Collected Letters of Edgar Allan Poe*, I:478–480 (Letter 190a).

Jan. 25. 45.

My Dear Sir,

Your letter of the 12fth reached me, in this city, only a few days ago. I am now living here.

I read the poem with great interest, and think it by much the best I have seen from your pen. Absolutely, also, I think it a remarkably fine poem. Some of the lines are, in all respects, admirable. For example—

Midnight in the silent city, midnight on the throbbing sea—
And the soft and silvery star-light fills the overhanging sky—
From the land beyond the ocean, on the rolling billows borne,

[62]

Comes the sunlight of the morning to the weary and the worn—
With the tribute and the treasure of the islands and the seas.

These are fine <u>verses</u>, independently of thought. Some of them are defective—for instance:

With foul shame to <u>the</u> weak-hearted, and the vanity of fear.

Your rhythm is trochaic—that is to say, composed of 2-syllable feet, in which the first is long, the second short. <u>With</u> and <u>the</u>, therefore are rhythmically long syllables, while naturally they are short. This contradiction should never exist. It exists in the line beginning—"With the tribute <u>and</u> the" &c. but not so glaringly. I am glad to see that you have altered "Oe'r the wild loud" into "Over the loud"; for, although <u>the</u> is improperly made long, you avoid the contraction of over. Upon the whole, you have a vivid conception of rhythm and you have no idea how much I mean in saying

(Over

<u>that.</u>

I may be in error, but I do not believe you will be able to <u>sell</u> the poem anywhere. Its merits are far higher than those of many poems that <u>are</u> sold for high prices; but what is paid for is the name of the poet. You are yet young as well in letters as in years. By and bye you may be able to make your own terms.

If <u>any</u>one will pay you for it, it will be Graham.

I would counsel you, however, to revise the whole carefully. "To <u>old</u> Bunker" is in bad taste. "E'en to build up," etc. is feeble—the contraction is bad. What do you mean by "like the river of a well"?—or by "the deepest scene of carnage"? You do not intend the scene to be d[eep] but the carnage. Deep, at best, is not the right epithet. The whole of the last stanza, I think, should be omitted, although its 3d line is excellent.

Very truly your friend

A.M. Ide Jr.   Edgar A Poe.

P.S. I shall very soon establish a Magazine in this city—"The Stylus".

N.B. "To their strong heart's muffled beating" will be immediately condemned as a plagiarism, from Longfellow's
"Our hearts like muffled drums are beating".

A few short years after his correspondence with Irving, Poe found himself on the opposite side of a similar exchange. In 1843, a farmer and aspiring poet from Massachusetts named Abijah M. Ide wrote to several prominent authors of the day, seeking "an acquaintance and fellowship with other Poets." In addition to Poe, he wrote letters to James Russell Lowell, Henry Wadsworth Longfellow, and editor John Neal. All three authors responded, and Neal published one of Ide's poems, alongside an endorsement of its author, in the newspaper *Brother Jonathan*.[71]

Lowell's correspondence with Ide was brief. Ide may have chosen Lowell in part because he was the editor of the literary journal the *Pioneer*, and his letter to Lowell (written on May 29, 1843) included a request that they be considered for publication. But the *Pioneer* had ceased publication after its third issue in March. Thus Lowell's letter is, first and foremost, a rejection letter. He gently dismisses Ide's poems, calling them "the first fruits of your muse" and "youthful poetry." He advises him: "you must not write till you have read . . . Read Shakespeare, Spenser, Milton, Wordsworth, Burns, Coleridge, Byron, Keats, & Shelley—they will tell you better than I whether you are a poet or not." Lowell concludes with a terse comment on "the failure of the 'Pioneer.'" If Ide was seeking fellowship, he was not to find it with Lowell.

Longfellow wrote more warmly and at greater length, offering several pieces of advice. First, he praises Ide's position as a farmer, encouraging him to "be both a farmer and a poet; and give us in your song, the scent of the wildflowers, and the new-turned soil, and the roar of the forest"—the classic writerly advice to "write what you know." He warns him against seeking fame, and encourages him to submit his work to monthly magazines and to read the works of Thomas Carlyle. He concludes by telling Ide to visit him if he is ever in Boston.

Ide seems to have attempted to take Longfellow up on this offer. Ide's second letter to the Boston author does not survive, but Longfellow's response to it on July 4, 1843 shows that Ide had attempted to find the author at the crowded dedication ceremony for a monument at Bunker Hill on June 17.[72] Longfellow also warns the young poet that he will be "at best a very poor and negligent correspondent." He concludes with additional recommendations for Ide's

71. Kent P. Ljungquist, "'Fellowship with Other Poets': Longfellow, Lowell, and Poe Correspond with A. M. Ide, Jr.," *Resources for American Literary Study* 28 (2002): 27–29.
72. Ibid., 34–35.

reading list: George Chapman's translation of Homer and Henry Francis Cary's translation of Dante. The tone of Longfellow's second letter to Ide is decidedly less warm than his first, though he does continue to offer the young author advice.

On October 1, 1843, Ide wrote to Edgar Allan Poe, sending him several poems for comment. Poe responded on October 19, warmly flattering the younger poet: "You ask me for my hand in friendship. I give it with the deepest sincerity. Had I met the few lines you send me, in any journal in the country, I should at once have felt myself the friend of their author—as I am unfeignedly of every man of genius." Lest this seem too high praise, he continues: "You well know that I am not given to flattery." Like Longfellow, Poe also advises against seeking fame, instead encouraging Ide to hone his craft and take whatever reputation his writing earns on its own merits. Poe continues that his current position gives him little ability to help Ide's career, but mentions that he is preparing to undertake a "bold and comprehensive enterprise"—he does not mention the name, but he is surely referring to his plans to start a literary journal of his own, to be called the *Stylus*.

In his initial letter to Ide, Poe encouraged him to "write me frequently and freely," and indeed the correspondence between the two, though relatively sparse, continued for more than a year. In January 1845, Ide sent his poem "Bunker's Hill" to Poe for comment. Poe's response on January 25 displays Poe's keen eye for the mechanics of poetry. Though calling the poem "by much the best I have seen from your pen," Poe dissects portions of the poem's rhythm, and does not mince words with his criticisms: he calls some of the lines "defective," "in bad taste," and "feeble." Despite the apparent harshness of some of these criticisms, Poe truly seems to admire the poem, and the letter's honest critique is far less harsh than much of Poe's published literary criticism. Moreover, Ide seems to have taken the critiques in their intended spirit, for many of the phrases to which Poe objects did not appear in the final version of "Bunker's Hill," published in the August 1845 issue of the *Knickerbocker*.[73]

73. Abijah M. Ide, Jr., "Bunker's Hill," *The Knickerbocker Magazine* 26, no. 2 (August 1845): 116–18.

Though Ide published few poems, he remained engaged in literature. He edited the *True Democrat* and the *Taunton Democrat*, in which he reprinted poems by Longfellow and Lowell. Editorial evidence for his opinion of Poe is somewhat less clear. In an 1850 notice of Rufus Griswold's edition of Poe's *Works* in the *Taunton Democrat*, unsigned but likely written by Ide, he praises the author's genius, but also declares "that Poe had established, as his own, a quite too severe standard of criticism, and weighed in his balance, everything was found wanting."[74] In these words we can sense the sting that Ide may have felt upon reading Poe's dissection of "Bunker's Hill." But the November 10, 1849 issue of the *True Democrat* includes a poem, also unsigned but likely from Ide's pen, entitled "Lines to the Memory of Edgar A. Poe, the Poet, Philosopher and Critic."

48⌉ WALT WHITMAN. *Leaves of Grass.* Brooklyn: [Fowler & Wells], 1856. Second edition. Publisher's green cloth; spine and cover gilt-lettered. Inscribed by Whitman to John Quincy Ward.

49⌉ WALT WHITMAN. Autograph letter signed ("Walt Whitman") to John Burroughs. St. Louis, January 2, 1880. 1 leaf, 2 pages 8½″ x 5⅜″. Published: Walt Whitman, *The Correspondence, volume III: 1876–1885.* Ed. Edwin Haviland Miller (New York: New York University Press, 1964), 172 (Letter 943).

> Jan 2 '80—
> 4½—PM
>
> Dear friend
>   Yours of 29th Dec with the present came safe to-day. Believe me I feel the gift, & it comes just right too—John please forward the enclosed slip to unknown friend—the above is a fair picture of the great Mississippi Bridge, ∧ East St Louis where I have loafed many hours—only it sets up much higher than the print gives—I don't

74. Quoted in Ljungquist, "'Fellowship with Other Poets': Longfellow, Lowell, and Poe Correspond with A. M. Ide, Jr.," 45.

48] Walt Whitman. *Leaves of Grass* (second edition, 1856).

believe there can be a grander thing of the kind on earth. –I leave here Sunday morning ^{Jan 4} at 8, on my return east, & shall be due in Philadelphia Monday evening, before 8—The last two or three weeks I have been well, for me, & am so now—

 —Your letter was deeply interesting to me. Made me see Emerson no doubt just as he is, the good pure soul — John I sympathize with you in the arm, & the treatment too—A great thaw & dense fog here as I write
Walt Whitman

Poe was not the only author to seek the assistance of an older writer at an early stage of his career. Shortly after the self-published first edition of *Leaves of Grass* appeared in 1855, Walt Whitman sent a copy of the book to Ralph Waldo Emerson, and the elder author replied with a kind letter of encouragement. Whitman was thrilled at the response, and—without Emerson's permission—submitted the letter for publication in the *New-York Tribune*. He began pasting the clipped-out letter into his remaining copies of *Leaves of Grass*, then incorporated it into *Leaves-Droppings*, a pamphlet collecting reviews of the book; lastly, he printed the letter along with his own long response (never actually sent to Emerson as a letter) into the second edition of the book in 1856.[75] On the spine of this edition, Whitman added a gilt-stamped quotation from Emerson's letter: "I greet you at the beginning of a great career – R.W. Emerson." English illustrator Frank Bellew, an acquaintance of both Emerson and Whitman, later recalled Emerson's anger at Whitman's presumption: "'In the New York 'Tribune'? No, no! impossible! he cannot have published it!' he exclaimed, with much surprise . . . 'Dear! Dear!' he muttered, 'that was very wrong, very wrong indeed. That was merely a private letter of congratulation.'"[76]

Despite Emerson's dismay at Whitman's actions, the two authors maintained a cordial relationship, and Emerson visited Whitman

75. Ed Folsom, "Transcendental Poetics: Emerson, Higginson, and the Rise of Whitman and Dickinson," in *The Oxford Handbook of Transcendentalism* (New York: Oxford University Press, 2010), 273.
76. Frank Bellew, "Recollections of Ralph Waldo Emerson," in *Emerson in His Own Time: A Biographical Chronicle of His Life, Drawn from Recollections, Interviews, and Memoirs by Family, Friends, and Associates*, ed. Ronald A. Bosco and Joel Myerson (Iowa City: University of Iowa Press, 2003), 149.

in Brooklyn a few months later, in December 1855. The two had infrequent contact following this, including a meeting in Boston in 1860 during which Emerson unsuccessfully attempted to convince Whitman to remove the *"Enfans d'Adam"* ("Children of Adam") poems from the third edition of *Leaves of Grass*, then in preparation.[77] In an 1880 letter to his own disciple, John Burroughs, Whitman described Emerson as a "good pure soul." In 1881, the year before Emerson's death, Whitman, Amos Bronson Alcott, and Louisa May Alcott spent a "blessed evening" at Emerson's home, where they discussed Henry Thoreau, Margaret Fuller, William Ellery Channing, and Horace Greeley.[78]

The immediate occasion for the 1880 letter containing Whitman's comment on Emerson illustrates another of his literary relationships. Though Whitman did not know it, "the present" referred to in the letter's opening came to him from the publisher James T. Fields, who had sent the poet (through Burroughs) $100 as a Christmas gift, insisting that it be given to the poet anonymously.[79]

The present copy of the 1856 edition of *Leaves of Grass* is inscribed by Whitman to his friend John Quincy Adams Ward, a popular New York-based sculptor known for works like his monument of George Washington at Federal Hall National Memorial in New York.

50] [SARAH HELEN WHITMAN]. RALPH WALDO EMERSON. *Essays*. Boston: James Munroe and Company, 1861. Black cloth. Sarah Helen Whitman's copy, with her signature on the title page and containing the calling card of "Mrs. R. W. Emerson" (Lidian Emerson) on the front paste-down.

77. Jerome Loving, "Emerson, Ralph Waldo (1803–1882)," ed. J. R. LeMaster and Donald D. Kummings, *Walt Whitman: An Encyclopedia* (New York: Routledge, 1998); Len Gougeon, "Emerson, Whitman, and Eros," *Walt Whitman Quarterly Review* 23, no. 3 (2006): 126–46, doi:10.13008/2153-3695.1797.
78. Walt Whitman, *Specimen Days & Collect* (Philadelphia: Rees Welsh & Co., 1883), 189.
79. Walt Whitman, *The Correspondence, Volume III: 1876–1885*, ed. Edwin Haviland Miller (New York: New York University Press, 1964), 172.

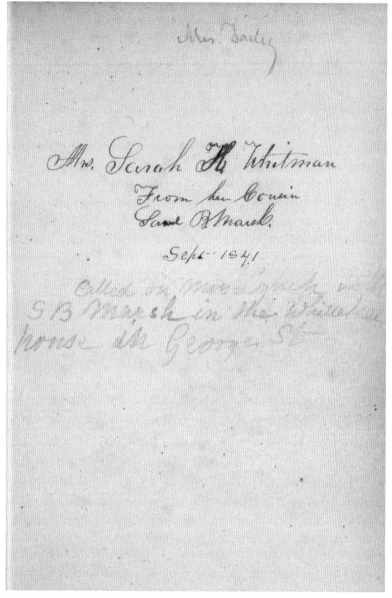

51] Inscription and pencil note in Sarah Helen Whitman's copy of *The Gift . . . for 1840*.

51⌉ [SARAH HELEN WHITMAN]. MISS LESLIE, ed. *The Gift: A Christmas Present and New Year's Present for 1840*. Philadelphia: Carey and Hart, [1839]. First edition. Original maroon morocco with bright, ornate gilt-stamped decorations and vignettes. Contains the first printing of "William Wilson" by Edgar Allan Poe. Sarah Helen Whitman's copy, with a gift inscription to her on the front free endpaper and her ownership signature on the engraved title page. BAL 16130 and 992.

52⌉ SARAH HELEN WHITMAN. *Edgar Poe and His Critics*. New York: Rudd & Carleton, 1860. First edition. BAL vol. 7, p. 146.

53⌉ SARAH HELEN WHITMAN. *Hours of Life, and Other Poems*. Providence: George H. Whitney, 1853. First edition. Original brown cloth decorated cover. Inscribed by Whitman to Poe's biographer John H. Ingram; with corrections to five poems in Whitman's hand; also with several ephemeral pieces laid in, two of which have manuscript annotations by Whitman.

Poet and critic Sarah Helen Whitman had numerous literary connections in New England. She was married to the poet John Winslow Whitman from 1828 until his death in 1833, and was a frequent guest at literary salons in Providence. She was friends with several prominent Transcendentalists, including Margaret Fuller and Ralph Waldo Emerson. (Evidence of Whitman's literary connections appears in her copy of Ralph Waldo Emerson's *Essays*, which contains a pasted-in calling card from "Mrs. R.W. Emerson"—Emerson's second wife, Lidian.) But she is perhaps best remembered for her connection to Edgar Allan Poe, and her prominent role in protecting his reputation in the years following his death.

Whitman first discovered Poe's writing in the 1840s. In an 1850 letter to Mary E. Hewitt, she described her first experience of reading his prose:

> I can never forget the impressions I felt in reading a story of his for the first time about six or seven years ago. I experienced a sensation of such intense horror that I dared neither look at anything he had written nor even utter his name. . . . By degrees this terror took the character of fascination — I devoured with a half-reluctant and fearful avidity every line that fell from his pen.[80]

There is no concrete evidence regarding which of Poe's tales Whitman first read, but one possibility is the story "William Wilson," first published in the 1840 edition of *The Gift*. Whitman received this book from her cousin, Samuel B. Marsh, in September 1841. Whitman's copy of *The Gift* contains marginal markings in three different sections of "William Wilson"—the only such marks in the volume— indicating not only that she read the story, but also that it made an impression.

The book also includes evidence concerning Whitman's literary life in Providence. Below the gift inscription from her cousin, the book contains a penciled note reading: "Called on Miss Lynch with S B Marsh in the Whittaker House in George St." The "Miss Lynch" referred to here is certainly Anne Lynch, who ran literary salons both in New York and at her mother's home in Providence. Whitman is known to have attended these salons, as did Ralph Waldo Emerson, Margaret Fuller, Louisa May Alcott, and others, including Edgar Allan Poe, who in 1845 read "The Raven" at one of Lynch's gatherings. At one of these salons in 1848, Lynch facilitated a meeting between Whitman and Poe.

Poe's strong personality made him a polarizing figure in the world of nineteenth-century literature. In life, he was well known for harsh literary criticism and his contentious relationships with other authors. His literary and personal feuds reached a fever pitch in 1846, and he was essentially driven out of New York literary society.

80. Sarah Helen Whitman, letter to Mary Hewitt, October 10, 1850. Quoted in Dwight Thomas, *The Poe Log: A Documentary Life of Edgar Allan Poe, 1809–1849*, American Authors Log Series (Boston: G. K. Hall, 1987), 614.

39] Henry David Thoreau. Autograph manuscript poem, "Inspiration," page 1 of 4.

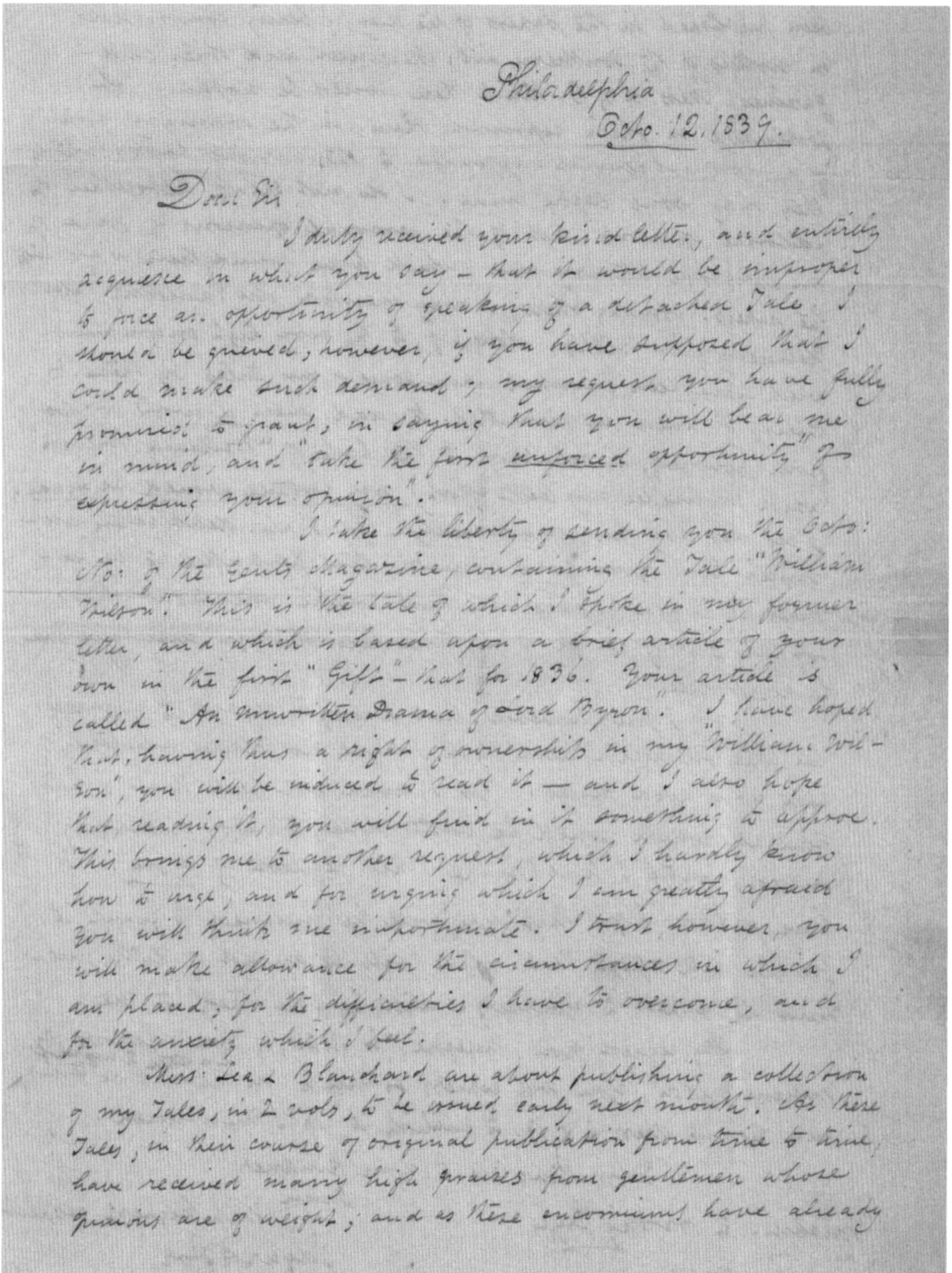

PLATE 6.
42] Edgar Allan Poe. Autograph letter signed to Washington Irving, October 12, 1839, page 1 of 2.

been published in the papers of the day, (being comprised in notices of the Southern Lit: Messenger and other Magazines) Mess. L & B. think there would be nothing objectionable in <u>their</u> reprinting them, in the ordinary form of an advertisement appended to the various books which they may issue before mine. I do not speak altogether of editorial opinions, but of the personal opinions of some of our principal literary men, which have found their way into the papers. Among others, I may mention Mr Paulding, Mr Kennedy & Mr Willis. Now, if, to the very high encomiums which have been lavished upon some of my tales by these & others, I could be permitted to add <u>even a word or two from yourself</u>, in relation to the tale of "William Wilson" (which I consider my best effort) <u>my fortune would be made.</u> I do not say this unadvisedly — for I am deliberately convinced that your good opinion, thus permitted to be expressed, would ensure me that public attention which would carry me on to fortune hereafter, by insuring me fame at once.

I feel, however, that I am, in regard to yourself an utter stranger — and that I have no claim whatever upon your good offices. Yet I could not feel that I had done all which could be justly done, towards ensuring success, until I had made this request of <u>you</u>. I have a strong hope that you will be inclined to grant it, for you will reflect that what will be an act of little moment in respect to yourself — will be life itself to me.

My request now, therefore, is that, if you approve of "William Wilson", you will express so much in a letter to myself in your own terms, and permit Mess. L & B. to publish it, as I mentioned.

Submitting all to your kindness

Washington Irving Esqr

I am with highest respects
Edgar A Poe

PLATE 7.
42] Edgar Allan Poe. Autograph letter signed to Washington Irving, October 12, 1839, page 2 of 2.

To Sarah.
Arranging her hair.

Oh, rich in _heart_! what matter, how
The silken tresses shade yr brow!
What matter, whether gem or rose
Or simple ribbon wreathe yr hair,
While that soft blush, so purely, glows,
While those dark eyes, such beauty, wear!

No rich array could lend your form,
Thus airy-light, one added charm;
No jewel, gift that girlish face,
With lovelier glow or softer grace
And he, who looks on you, with eyes
Where all his _soul_ to yrs replies,
Is prouder of you, simply so,
Than when adorned yr graces glow;
And joys to know, his fairy flower
Can gaily bloom, in Home's sweet bower,

PLATE 8.
54] Frances Sargent Osgood. Autograph manuscript poem, "To Sarah, Arranging Her Hair," page 1 of 2.

Writing to Whitman on January 31, 1848, Lynch commented on Poe's reputation: "There was a great war in *bluestockingdom* some time ago & Poe did not behave very honorably in it — the truth is that with all his genius he has no moral sense, & he said & did a great many things that were very abominable."[81] Lynch is here referring to the events surrounding Poe's expulsion from the New York literary scene in 1846. Already a polarizing figure, Poe found himself enmeshed in a scandal over his close relationships with two married women (both authors themselves): Frances Sargent Osgood and Elizabeth Ellet. The gossip surrounding Poe escalated, and he wound up in a brief fistfight with Thomas Dunn English, editor of the *Aristidean.* Following this scuffle, Poe was no longer welcome at New York salons.

Despite Lynch's word of caution, Whitman continued to express interest in meeting Poe, and read a Valentine's poem for him at one of Lynch's salons. (Poe was not invited to the event.) The two met in person that fall, and were soon engaged, on the condition that Poe stop drinking. He was unable to keep this vow, and Whitman broke off the engagement after only a few weeks.

Poe's reputation declined further after his death. Rufus Griswold, a literary editor with whom Poe had quarreled, immediately wrote a lengthy obituary for the *New-York Tribune* in which he declared that Poe had "few or no friends." Despite their feud, Poe had named Griswold his literary executor, and Griswold expanded his obituary into a slanderous memoir of Poe's life in his edition of Poe's *Works*, published in 1856. This biographical sketch, which includes fabricated correspondence and other demonstrable falsehoods, depicts the author as a cruel drunkard and a raving madman, and would damage Poe's reputation for decades to come.

Whitman took Griswold's declaration that Poe had "no friends" as a challenge. In 1860, she published *Edgar Poe and His Critics*, a defense of Poe's reputation. In her preface, Whitman explicitly refers to Griswold's depiction of Poe as a friendless outsider: "It has been assumed by a recent English critic that 'Edgar Poe had no friends.'

81. Anne C. Lynch to Sarah Helen Whitman, January 31, 1848. Quoted in ibid., 719.

As an index to a more equitable and intelligible theory of the idio-syncrasies of his life, and as an earnest protest against the spirit of Dr. Griswold's unjust memoir, these pages are submitted to his more candid readers and critics by ONE OF HIS FRIENDS."[82]

Another figure who was essential in the resuscitation of Poe's rep-utation was the English biographer John Henry Ingram, who wrote the first full-length biography of Poe and edited a four-volume edi-tion of his works in 1874–1875. In thanks for his efforts on behalf of Poe's memory, Whitman gave Ingram a copy of her 1853 book of poetry, *Hours of Life*, with a gift inscription reading: "To J H Ingram with the grateful acknowledgements of Sarah Helen Whitman."

54] FRANCES SARGENT OSGOOD. Autograph let-ter signed ("Frances S. Osgood") to Sarah [Elliott], with autograph manuscript poem, "To Sarah, Arranging Her Hair." [Undated, ca. 1840–1849.] Single leaf, 3 pages, 9½″ x 7¾″. With integral address panel.

> Dear Sarah,
> The lines were suggested the other night at your house. I did not write them in the <u>book</u>, because I have made a resolution never to write in Albums. – I̶f̶ ̶I̶ Don't paste it in—if you love me!—
> With my affectionate regards to your husband, & my warmest thanks for all your & his kindness to the Wanderer,
>   I remain,
>   Yrs truly & always,
>   Frances S. Osgood.

This letter (plate 8) from the poet Frances Sargent Osgood shows the literary side of a non-literary friendship. The identity of the re-cipient of the letter and poem is not known. She is identified only by her first name, and the letter is addressed to "Albert Elliott"—prob-ably Sarah's husband, referred to in the letter. As a preface to the poem, Osgood tells the dedicatee that "I did not write [the poem] in the <u>book</u>, because I have made a resolution never to write in Albums. <u>Don't</u> paste it in – if you love me!"

82. Sarah Helen Whitman, *Edgar Poe and His Critics* (New York: Rudd & Car-leton, 1860), [vii].

Friendship albums were common throughout the nineteenth century, as a place for people—most frequently women—to collect "autographs, poetry, prose, and wishes from friends."[83] Scrapbooks are vital records of how people in the nineteenth century viewed themselves and the world around them. Some such albums have played a major role in American literature: much of Emily Dickinson's work was written in scrapbooks, alongside ephemera from her daily life.[84]

The reason for Osgood's vow "never to write in Albums" is not entirely clear. But the charming tone of this poem exudes friendship, and well represents Poe's conclusion: "About everything she writes we perceive this indescribable and incomprehensible charm."[85] The poem first appeared in her collection of *Poems* in 1846, and was reprinted in the longer collection of the same title published in 1850; Osgood died of tuberculosis that same year.

55] ALICE CARY. Autograph letter signed ("Alice Cary") to Mr. [George Palmer?] Putnam. [New York]: January 19, [between 1855–1871]. 2 pages, 8″ x 5″. Accompanied by a *carte-de-visite* portrait of Alice Cary.

> 53 East 20th St
> Jan 19.

Dear Mr. Putnam—I send a prose sketch, with this, which has the merit, if no other, of being almost literally true. The bracelet came into my possession just as I have stated, and indeed I have done little more than change names and places, through out. Most of the characters are living within a few blocks of me. The Bracelet belonged to the wife of Edgar A. Poe, and of course Poe himself is the person whose visits to the second hand shop are set forth in the sketch.

I also send you some verses. Allow me to say that ~~my~~ [illegible deletion] ~~over~~ I receive from twenty five to fifty dollars from the newspapers, for my poems, and cannot therefore name a lower

83. Katherine Ott, Susan Tucker, and Patricia P. Buckler, "An Introduction to the History of Scrapbooks," in *The Scrapbook in American Life* (Philadelphia: Temple University Press, 2006), 7.

84. Ibid., 19–20.

85. Edgar Allan Poe, "[Review of] 'A Wreath of Wild Flowers from New England' [and] 'Poems' by Frances Sargent Osgood," in *The Complete Works of Edgar Allan Poe, Vol. 13: Literary Criticism, Vol. 6*, ed. James A. Harrison, vol. 13 (New York: Thomas Y. Crowell, 1902), 114.

price to you than twenty five. I will send my servant to you Saturday morning, and if you prefer to decline my contributions please return the mss by ~~my~~ him. I keep that you will examine, therefore, and decide before that time.

With all good wishes
I am truly yours,
Alice Cary.

Alice Cary and her sister Phoebe were minor but well-connected poets. Born in Ohio, the sisters began writing poetry in their teens, and earned the praise of critics like Edgar Allan Poe, Horace Greeley, and John Greenleaf Whittier. Rufus Griswold included the sisters in his 1848 anthology *The Female Poets of America,* and in 1850 an anthology of their work appeared under the title *Poems of Alice and Phoebe Cary.* In 1855, Alice relocated to New York City, and for the rest of her life she and her sister hosted literary salons in her home. Regular attendees included Greeley; Whittier; Richard and Elizabeth Stoddard; Mary Booth, editor of *Harper's Bazaar*; William Lloyd Garrison; and P. T. Barnum.[86]

In this letter addressed to "Mr. Putnam"—likely George Palmer Putnam, whose publishing house Wiley and Putnam issued works by major American authors like Edgar Allan Poe and Herman Melville—Alice discusses a prose sketch concerning a bracelet that once belonged to Virginia Poe. This sketch does not appear in any of Cary's publications, and may no longer be extant. However, Cary also wrote a letter mentioning "The Bracelet" to James T. Fields, co-proprietor of Ticknor and Fields and publisher of the *Atlantic Monthly.* In this letter she also mentions her hopes to write more on Poe and his wife.[87]

Cary's letter shows Poe's growing role as a literary figure in the years following his death, as represented by a well-connected figure in the New York literary community to which Poe himself had belonged.

---

86. June Edwards, "The Cary Sisters," *Dictionary of Unitarian and Universalist Biography* (The Unitarian Universalist History & Heritage Society, March 20, 2003), http://uudb.org/articles/carysisters.html (acccessed May 8, 2017).
87. Alice Cary, "Letter to James T. Fields," July 28, [no year], 6978-d, University of Virginia Library, Special Collections.

Hartford, Conn.t April 22d 1839.

My dear Sir;

I thank you for your letter, and
remembrances by Mr. Ripley. Mary, my little
daughter of ten years old, returns you her thanks,
for the engravings you were so kind as to
send her, which are a source of much pleasure
to her, and her companions. — I was pleased
to find among them, your own likeness, & also
to trace its resemblance to a friend of ours, the
Rev.d Dr. Wainwright, of New-York, who is a
native of your island. —

I send you a copy of
my "Girl's Reading Book," and if you have
republished any of my works, of a later
date than "Letters to Young Ladies," should
like to receive a copy of them. I am a little
fastidious about the style of execution of what
I have written, feeling that they are not of so
great innate power, as to be independent of the
influence derived from a handsome exterior.
You will say, that the one I now send, rather
contradicts this sentiment. But the Publisher
who was at a distance, disappointed me, and

framed it only on the principle of wide and cheap circulation among schools. Nine editions have appeared, during the last year, and I am now printing a 12mo myself, to be more agreeable to my own eye.

Wishing you grace to wield these two great engines, the Press & the Pulpit, for the honour of our Master, the conversion of many, and the eternal health of your own soul, I remain

yours, with true christian regard,

L. H. Sigourney. —

P.S. Will you please to give the enclosed to Mr Rittick?

56] Lydia Huntley Sigourney. Autograph letter signed to Rev. Joseph Belcher, April 22, 1839, page 2 of 2.

CHAPTER FIVE
Women Authors and Their Publishers

56] LYDIA HUNTLEY SIGOURNEY. Autograph letter signed ("L.H. Sigourney") to Rev. Joseph Belcher. Hartford, April 22, 1839. 2 pages, 10″ x 8″. With integral address panel.

Hartford, Conn.t April 22nd 1839.

My dear Sir,

I thank you for your letter, and remembrances by Mr. Ripley. Mary, my little daughter of ten years old, returns you her thanks for the engravings you were so kind as to send her, which are a source of much pleasure to her, and her companions. I was pleased to find among them, your own likeness, & also to trace its resemblance to a friend of ours, the Rev.d Dr. Wainwrights, of New York, who is a native of your islands.

I send you a copy of my "Girl's Reading Book," and if you have re-published any of my works, of a later date than "Letters to Young Ladies," should like to receive a copy of them. I am a little fastidious about the style of execution of what I have written, feeling that they are not of so great innate power, as to be independent of the influence derived from a handsome exterior. You will say, that the one I now send, rather contradicts this sentiment. But the Publisher who was at a distance, disappointed me, and framed it only on the principle of wide and cheap circulation among schools. Nine editions have appeared, during the last year, and I am now printing a 12mo myself, to be more agreeable to my own eye.

Wishing you grace to wield those two great engines, the Press & the Pulpit, for the honour of our Master, the conversion of many, and the eternal health of your own soul, I remain

Yours, with true Christian regard,

L.H. Sigourney.

PS. Will you please to give the enclosed to Mr. Killick?

Lydia Huntley Sigourney began her career in obscurity, writing anonymously and even smuggling proof sheets of her writings through friends so that her husband wouldn't find out about them.[88] Her name became publicly known after the publication of her popular *Letters to Young Ladies*, and the failure of her husband's business put increasing financial pressure on the family. Sigourney became a prolific and popular author, penning dozens of books and becoming one of the first and most successful American woman authors of the nineteenth century.

In this letter (plates 9-10), Sigourney writes to her English editor, Rev. Joseph Belcher, who had published English editions of her works, including the English edition of *Letters to Young Ladies* and a volume of her selected poetry entitled *Lays From the West*. Sigourney sent with this letter a copy of her *Girl's Reading Book*, which had been published by J. Orville Taylor in 1838. The book, along with the accompanying *Boy's Reading Book*, earned Sigourney a royalty of ten cents per copy, and both were widely distributed in schools.[89] By way of apology for the inexpensive production of the *Girl's Reading Book*, Sigourney expresses her care regarding the physical appearance of her books. However, her plan to reissue a more attractive edition of the *Girl's Reading Book* does not seem to have come to fruition: it went into several editions from multiple publishers, but all used the same basic, utilitarian design.

57] SARAH J. HALE. Autograph letter signed ("S.J. Hale") to James Munroe & Co. Philadelphia, Dec. 18, 1850. 1 page, 8¾" x 7⅞". With integral address leaf in Hale's hand. Docketed by Munroe.

Philadelphia; Dec. 18, 1850

James Munroe Esq.—

I send you a copy of the "Lady's Book" for Jan. 1851—and also of *Nov. 1850—which contains notices of several books you forwarded me. There will be other notices in Feby.

Whatever books you send, please envelope and direct to <u>me</u>, care of Mr. Godey, if you please, and I will exm. and notice as early as possible.

Very truly yours
S.J. Hale

88. Gordon S. Haight, *Mrs. Sigourney, the Sweet Singer of Hartford* (New Haven: Yale University Press, 1930), 34.
89. Ibid., 39.

Sarah J. Hale was one of the most extraordinary and influential women in the American literary world of the nineteenth century. She was the founding editor of the *Ladies' Magazine*, begun in 1828, in which she regularly advocated for the education of women. This magazine was purchased by Louis A. Godey in 1837, who combined it with his own *Lady's Book*, with Hale continuing as editor until she retired in 1877, at the age of 89. Under her editorship, *Godey's Lady's Book* published works by Edgar Allan Poe, Nathaniel Hawthorne, Oliver Wendell Holmes, Washington Irving, Lydia H. Sigourney, Frances Sargent Osgood, and innumerable others. She also wrote the poem "Mary Had a Little Lamb" and successfully advocated for the establishment of a Thanksgiving holiday.[90]

This letter to Boston publisher James Munroe & Company links Hale to an important publisher. Munroe issued works by many New England authors, including Ralph Waldo Emerson's *Nature* and *Essays*, Henry David Thoreau's *A Week on the Concord and Merrimack Rivers*, Amos Bronson Alcott's *The Doctrine and Discipline of Human Culture*, and William Ellery Channing's *Works*. Munroe also published the first American edition of Thomas Carlyle's *Sartor Resartus*, arranged by Ralph Waldo Emerson.

In this letter, Hale sends two issues of *Godey's Lady's Book* to Munroe, one of which—the November 1850 issue—contained notices for several of Munroe's publications, including William Ware's *American Unitarian Biography* and Catharine M. A. Cowper's *Lucy's Half-Crown; or, the Art of Making People Happy Without Money*. A year earlier, in its September 1849 issue, the *Lady's Book* had printed a positive notice of Thoreau's *A Week on the Concord and Merrimack Rivers*: "It is just the book to read in the idleness of summer, when wishing to enjoy the pleasures of journeying, without the inconvenience which the actual packing up and going off in hot steamboats and dusty cars occasion. Read it, and see."[91]

90. For a brief summary of Hale's career, see Frank Luther Mott, *A History of American Magazines, 1741-1850*. Cambridge, Mass.: The Belknap Press of Harvard University Press, 1966, p. 349–350 and 582–593.
91. "Editors' Book Table." *Godey's Lady's Book*, September 1849, p. 223.

58⌉ LOUISA MAY ALCOTT. *Little Men: Life at Plumfield with Jo's Boys.* Boston: Roberts Brothers, 1871. First edition. Red cloth lettered in gilt. From the library of Frederick Alcott Pratt, with his stamp on the dedication page and signature and note on the front pastedown: "F. Alcott Pratt. 1ˢᵗ edition. Keep." Also with a presentation inscription dated 1933 on the front blank, likely in the hand of Frederick's widow, Jessica Cate Pratt.

Louisa May Alcott came from a literary background: her father, Amos Bronson Alcott, was an educator and a Transcendentalist, and her schooling included lessons from his friends and acquaintances, among them Ralph Waldo Emerson and Henry David Thoreau, as well as associations with Nathaniel Hawthorne, Margaret Fuller, and others. Her debut novel, *Little Women*, was a success, inspiring two sequels, including this novel, *Little Men*.

Little Men bears the dedication: "To Freddy and Johnny, The Little Men to whom she owes some of the best and happiest hours of her life, this book is gratefully dedicated by their loving 'Aunt Weedy.'" The "Freddy" of the dedication is Alcott's nephew, Frederick Alcott Pratt, the basis for the character John "Demi" Brooke, from whose library the present copy originates. Alcott supported Frederick and his brother, John Sewall Pratt, following the untimely death of their father John Bridge Pratt in 1870, and wrote this novel with the intention of generating income for the Pratt family.[92] In addition to this close family connection, this novel contains an important literary connection as well: the character of Professor Bhaer is modeled on Emerson.[93]

59⌉ LOUISA MAY ALCOTT. Autograph letter signed ("L.M. Alcott") to Mr. [Alexander] Drake. [N.p.]: September 11, [1877?]. 3 pages on a single folded leaf, 5″x 3⅞″.

92. Gregory Eiselein, "Pratt, Frederick Alcott, and Pratt, John Sewall," ed. Gregory Eiselein and Anne K. Phillips, *The Louisa May Alcott Encyclopedia* (Westport, Conn.: Greenwood Press, 2001), 265–66.
93. Mary Lamb Shelden, "Emerson, Ralph Waldo," ed. Gregory Eiselein and Anne K. Phillips, *The Louisa May Alcott Encyclopedia* (Westport, Conn.: Greenwood Press, 2001), 97.

Sept 11th-

Mr Drake

Dear Sir.

    Mrs. Dodge writes me that she has not heard from F.B. Sanborn about his sketch in the Hearth & Home.

    To save time I send one which includes all the facts of my interest, & a portion of Mr. Sanborn's, as I have no copy of that.

    Mrs. D. speaks of your attempts to get an agreeable picture out of the bad photographs I sent her.

    If I thought I could do any better I would have some taken, but I am sure I shall never get a cheerful face while the sun paints me so will not waste time.

              Respectfully
                L.M. Alcott

Alcott was careful regarding her image, as illustrated by this letter to the art editor of the juvenile magazine *St. Nicholas*. In many of the extant portraits of Alcott, she appears thoughtful, occasionally to the point of seeming mournful or morose. This letter indicates that she was aware of the problem: "I am sure I shall never get a cheerful face while the sun paints me." Nevertheless, she clearly hopes to be represented by the best possible image. She refers Drake to the image of her that appeared on the cover of the January 16, 1875 issue of *Hearth & Home*. A relatively cheerful portrait of Alcott appeared in the December 1877 issue of *St. Nicholas*, accompanying Franklin Sanborn's flattering profile "Miss Alcott. The Friend of Little Women and of Little Men."

60⌉ JULIA WARD HOWE. Autograph postcard signed ("Julia W. Howe") to J[eanette] L[eonard] Gilder. [Boston], April 14, 1881. 1 page, 3″ x 5⅛″. Addressed in Howe's hand.

    129 M^{nt} Vernon St. Ap^l 19th/81
    Dear Editor, you shall have Hawthorne early next week, & [him?] next, or vice versa.
        Yr's truly
            Julia W. Howe.

Julia Ward Howe was a prominent author, activist, and abolitionist, and is best remembered today as the author of "The Battle Hymn of the Republic." In this postcard from late in her career, she writes to Jeanette Gilder, a trailblazing female journalist who co-founded and edited the literary magazine the *Critic*. In the span of a few short words, Howe updates Gilder on the status of two pieces for the *Critic:* the first, referred to as simply "Hawthorne" in the postcard, is "Two Glimpses of Hawthorne," which appeared in the June 18, 1881 issue, and recounts Howe's visit to Hawthorne's "Old Manse" in 1845. Howe contrasts this early meeting with another encounter later in his career, after he had established his reputation, but notes both Hawthorne's kindness to her and his sensitivity: "Whenever [his eyes'] look encountered mine, they seemed to say: 'This sensitive soul prays the world not to be rough or rude.'"[94] The other piece referred to in this brief note is not clear: Howe's other works in the *Critic* in the late spring of 1881 include "Life and Education of Laura Bridgman" (May 7) and "The Greek Play at Cambridge" (May 21, a review of a performance of *Oedipus Tyrannus*).

61] HARRIET BEECHER STOWE. Autograph letter signed ("Harriet Beecher Stowe") to Frederick Mitchell Munroe. Hartford, December 20, 1892. 1 page, 8˝ x 5˝. With original envelope addressed in Stowe's hand.

> Hartford Dec 20 1892
> Mr Munroe
> Dear Sir. I wish to thank the gentlemanly editors of "Brooklyn Life", for their kindness in so long sending me their paper. From its opening number, I believe it has been a great source of amusement & diversion to me, & often, also brings me tidings of Brooklyn friends. I hail its arrival, each Saturday morning, with pleasure. Among its pleasant & friendly pages I have whiled away many an hour that otherwise would have been dull and tedious.
> Please accept my best wishes for a successful New Year both for yourselves and your paper.
> Sincerely Yours. Harriet Beecher Stowe

94. Julia Ward Howe, "Two Glimpses of Hawthorne," *The Critic* 1, no. 12 (June 18, 1881): 158.

Harriet Beecher Stowe was one of the most successful authors of the nineteenth century. Her novel *Uncle Tom's Cabin* was the best-selling work of fiction in America prior to the Civil War, and her later works sold well and circulated widely.

Frederick Mitchell Munroe, co-founder and editor of the weekly *Brooklyn Life*, was part of a family with numerous literary connections. His brother, Kirk Munroe, was editor of *Harper's Young People* and the author of over thirty books for boys. His younger sister, Charlotte Elizabeth Munroe Putnam, was married to Herbert Putnam, the eighth Librarian of Congress. His eldest sister, Susan Mitchell Munroe Stowe, had a direct connection to Harriet Beecher Stowe: she was married to Harriet's son, Charles E. Stowe.

This letter shows Frederick Munroe using this family connection to enhance his newspaper's reputation. Munroe had given Stowe a free subscription to the *Brooklyn Life*, and in this effusive letter Stowe writes to Munroe about her enjoyment of the weekly. The tone of the letter indicates that it was likely intended as a "blurb" for Munroe to use in advertising for his newspaper. Stowe and her family were well known in Brooklyn: she had lived there in the 1860s, and her brother, Henry Ward Beecher, was a prominent Congregationalist minister there. This endorsement of her relative's publication draws on her role as both a national and a local celebrity.

62] ANNA KATHARINE GREEN. Autograph letter signed ("Anna Katherine Rohlfs") to [A. A.] Hill of the American Press Association. Buffalo, New York, [ca. 1894–1895]. 2 pages, 7⅞″ x 4⅞″.

> 29 Highland Ave
> Buffalo N.Y.

Dear Mr Hill

Yours of the 25th is before me. The price asked for story is less than a successful story is worth and less than I have received ~~from~~ for some of my best work.

Your business being quite different from the ordinary methods, I am not in a position to know what you could get out of the story in profit.

I want you to have the story if you see any advantage in it for the American Press Ass'n. If you will therefore frankly state what you would be willing to give for it, especially for serial purposes, I will let you know by return mail if I can meet the price and conditions.

Yours truly

Anna Katharine Rohlfs

In the latter half of the nineteenth century, many daily newspapers began to rely on "plate-service" companies, which would provide stereotype plates of news, fiction, and other general-interest matter to a wide range of local newspapers. Hundreds of publications across the country were able to fill out their pages with this syndicated material, thereby reducing the need for writing original material. One of the largest of these "boilerplate" syndicates was the American Press Association, which made efforts to obtain original fiction and poetry, as well as reprinting material first published elsewhere. According to Charles Johanningsmeier, the term "boilerplate" may have originated "from a printers' joke about the Association's shop being in the same building as an iron foundry." Though the association largely relied on unsolicited manuscripts, and thus attracted few established authors, many of their contributors became well-known names, including Stephen Crane, Charlotte Perkins Gilman, and Jack London.[95]

A letter from pioneering mystery novelist Anna Katharine Green (signed with her married name, Rohlfs) to the APA suggests one reason that the syndicate may have failed to attract submissions from established authors: low pay rates. Writing to "Mr. Hill," almost certainly the APA's managing editor A. A. Hill, Green makes it clear that the APA had offered her less than she considered her work worth. She seems somewhat baffled by the company, stating that the APA's model is "quite different from the ordinary methods."

This letter likely relates to the story "Midnight in Beauchamp Row," an 1895 tale syndicated by the APA. Green was an established author by this point, having published over a dozen novels, but the

95. Charles Johanningsmeier, *Fiction and the American Literary Marketplace: The Role of Newspaper Syndicates in America, 1860-1900*. Cambridge: Cambridge University Press, 2002, p. 43. For more on plate-service companies in general, and the APA in particular, see Johanningsmeier, p. 42–48.

letter indicates this was her first time dealing with a plate-service business. The exact terms struck for this story are not known, but the reference to serial publication suggests that "Beauchamp Row" may not have been the story originally submitted to the APA; at fewer than 5,000 words, it is too brief for serialization. It is possible that Green accepted the price offered by Hill, but only for a shorter work. This letter suggests the changing landscape of periodical publication at the close of the nineteenth century, as well as demonstrating Green's business acumen.

CHAPTER SIX

"Goodly harvests which ripen late": Herman Melville's English Publishers

---

63] HERMAN MELVILLE. Autograph letter signed ("Herman Melville") to John Brodhead. New York, December 30, 1846. 4 pages, 9¾″ x 7″. Published: Herman Melville, *Correspondence.* Ed. Lynn Horth (Evanston: Northwestern University Press, 1993), 70–71.

New York Dec 30[th] 1846

John Rom[e]yn Brodhead Esq.

Dear Sir:— The longstanding acquaintance between our families, and particularly that between my late brother Mr. Gansevoort Melville and yourself, induce me to solicit a favor which my own slight acquaintance with you would not perhaps warrant. By granting it, as I think you will, you will confer that which I shall not forget.

I have recently made an arrangement with the Harpers to bring out a new work of mine. But altho' it has just gone to press, they are to defer publication until I have concluded arrangements to bring out the work in England. This is for the express purpose, as you will perceive, of securing a copyright there. — Now, I have no correspondent in London who can act for me—is it too much to solicit your friendly offices? — There is little to be done—a mere sale to effect— that accomplished, the rest remains with the publisher.

Presuming that you will not refuse what I ask, permit me, Dear Sir, to take it for granted.

Mr. Murray of Albemarle Street has by letter informed me, that upon receiving the proof sheets of my new book he would make me a liberal offer therefore. — I, of course, guaranteeing the integrity of the copyright for England, which I will do.

Now, relying upon your friendly consent to do what I ask of you, I shall ∧ [write] Mr. Murray to the effect, that I shall empower Mr. Brodhead to treat with him for the sale of the book, & that I will also send the proof sheets under cover to you by the steamer of the 1st of

February, & that you will upon their arrival at once submit them to him for an offer.

Do not, I pray you, entertain the slightest apprehension or delicacy as to any responsibility you may think you will assume by acting for me in this matter. For by the steamer which carries over the proof sheets I will give you such instructions as will remove all scruples upon this head.

I will write you fully by the steamer of the 1st of February.

You see, I rely upon your granting this favor — Your declining so to do will not only place me ∧ in a very unple[a]sant predicament, but will occasion me no small pecuniary loss.

With high consideration and true regard, Bel[i]eve Me, Dear Sir
Your obedient Servant
Herman Melville

Should there be any probability of your being out of town upon the arrival of the proof sheets, I must beg of you to leave directions for having them forthwith forwarded to Mr Murray. I shall write him to this effect.

64⌉ JOHN R. BRODHEAD. Autograph letter signed ("John R. Brodhead") to Harnden & Co. London, February 18, 1847. 3 pages, 8⅞"x 7⅜". Published: John H. Birss, ed., "'A Mere Sale to Effect' with Letters of Herman Melville," *New Colophon* 1, no. part 3 (July 1948), 242.

90 Eaton Square
18 February 1847

Gentlemen,

I have just received your letter of yesterday in which you state, that by the "Hibernia" steamer, you received from your Boston house, a parcel addressed to me, "which on being examined at the Customs, was found to contain an American reprint of an English Author, entitled 'a Narrative of a voyage to the North Seas by Melville',—and as such. . . was seized by the "Examining officer."
~~I am not acquainted with any such English work as that the w~~

By the same Steamer, I received a letter from Mr Harman [*sic*] Melville of New York, in which he states that he has forward to me, through your house, ∧ a parcel containing the proof sheets of an Original work of which he is the Author, entitled "Omoo, a narrative of Adventures in the South Seas,"—and though in your letter you describe the parcel seized by the Custom House Officer to be "a Narrative of a voyage to the North seas by Melville", ∧ ~~a suspected English work~~ (which the officer pronounced to be an American reprint of an English Author) I presume it is actually the parcel containing the identical proof sheets forwarded to me by Mr Melville of New York.

If this be so, it is an ∧ unpublished, and altogether original American work, and so far from its being a reprint of an English work, by an English Author, it has never been published at all. Either in England or America. ~~The proof sheets were sent to me by Mr Melville, for~~ [illegible] ~~the author,~~

The Custom's Officer therefore, who ∧ in the superabundance of his zeal without knowledge made the ∧ deliberate seizure of the proof sheets of an Original and unpublished American work, under the pretence ~~that it was~~ of its being an American reprint of an English work, has not only displayed great ignorance (~~and incompetency to his work,~~) but has unjustifiably transcended his duty, ~~and exposed himself to the consequences of his act.~~)

I have to request that you will immediately on the receipt of this take the proper ~~measu~~ steps to have the parcel ~~in question~~ ∧ thus wrongly seized delivered up to you, and that you will forward it at once to Mr John Miller, No 26 Henrietta St. Covent Garden, London, the Despatch Agent of this Legation, to whom I have delivered the Bill of Lading you sent me.

I have also to request that you will ~~send~~ communicate to me the name of the officer who ~~has displayed~~ ~~whose~~ ~~made this wrongful and most inexcusable~~ offensive so improperly seized and detained the parcel. ~~conduct, deserves has acted in this wrongful and~~ [illegible] ~~offensive manner.~~

I am, Gentlemen,
Your obedient Servant
John R. Brodhead
Secretary of the
United States Legation.
—

[At foot of first page:]

Messrs Harnden & Co
Liverpool

65⎤ JOHN R. BRODHEAD. Autograph letter signed ("John R. Brodhead") to John Murray. London, February 20, 1847. 1 page, 9⅜″ x 7⅝″. Published: Birss, ed., "A Mere Sale to Effect," 243.

90 Eaton Square.
20 February. 1847.

Dear Sir.

I send you herewith, ~~the~~ for your examination and ~~opinion~~ decision, the proof sheets of Mr Herman Melville's new work, "Omoo, a Narrative of Adventures in the South Seas"; which I have this day received, through Harnden's Express, and ∧ ^{to which I beg your early attention.} ~~am~~

    I am, Dear Sir,

        very truly yours
        John R. Brodhead

John Murray, Esq
Albemarle St.

66⌉ JOHN MURRAY. Autograph letter signed ("John Murray") to John R. Brodhead. London, February 26, [1847]. 2 pages, 7″ x 4¼″. Published: Birss, ed., "A Mere Sale to Effect," 243.

        Albemarle St
        Feb. 26

Dear Sir or Madam: I am much pleased with ∧ ^{Omoo—} Herman Melville's new work. Though it has not the novelty of the former it is full of talent & interest.

    I shall be happy to give, for the copyright of it in this country, the sum of One Hundred & Fifty Pounds—payable £100. by note at eight months from the day of publication, & £50. by cheque at 12 months date from the first publication.

    If these conditions appear such as you can accept, I will under take to bring out the English Edition on or before the 1st of April I shall thereupon take it for granted that the book will not be published in America until that day.

    With thanks for your kindness in placing the work in my hands

        I remain dear Sir
        Your obliged & faithful
        John Murray

John Romeyn Brodhead Esq
&   &   &

67⌉ JOHN MURRAY. Autograph letter signed ("John Murray") to John R. Brodhead. London, March 1, [1847].

1 page, 7″ x 4¼″. Published: Birss, ed., "A Mere Sale to Effect," 244.

Albemarle St

March 1

Dear Sir

   Conformably with your suggestion, I agree, instead of paying for the copyright of Mr. Herman Melvilles new book £150.. at 8 & 12 mo's,- to pay you at once, on the publication £144..3..4- in cash being the above named sum deducting the customary interest

   I remain Dear Sir

Yours very respectfully

John Murray

J.R. Brodhead Esq

68⌉ HERMAN MELVILLE. Autograph letter signed ("H. Melville") to Richard Bentley. New York, July 20, 1849. 3 pages, 9¾″ x 7″. Published: Melville, *Correspondence*, 133–134; Birss, ed., "A Mere Sale to Effect," 247–248.

New York July 20ᵗʰ '49

Dear Sir — I am indebted to you for yours of the 20ᵗʰ June. — Your report concerning "Mardi" was pretty much as I expected; but you know perhaps that there are goodly harvests which ripen late, especially when the grain is remarkably strong. At any rate, Mʳ Bentley, let us by all means lay this flattering unction to our souls, since it is so grateful a prospect to you as a publisher, & to me as an author. — But I need not assure you how deeply I regret that, for any period, you should find this venture of "Mardi" an unprofitable thing for you; & I should feel more grieved, did I suppose it was going to eventuate in a positive loss to you. But this can not be in the end. — However, these considerations—all, solely with respect to yourself—prevail upon me to accept your amendment to my overtures concerning my new work:—which amendment, I understand to be thus—£100 down on the receipt of the sheets, an account of half profits; & that you shall be enabled to publish ∧ ᵃ ᶠᵉʷ ᵈᵃʸˢ previous to the appearance of the book in America—and this, I hereby guarantee.

   The work is now going thro' the press, & I think I shall be able to send it to you in the course of three weeks or so. It will readily make two volumes got up in your style, as I have enlarged it somewhat to the size of "Omoo"—perhaps it may be a trifle larger.

   Notwithstanding the recent decision of your courts of law, I can hardly imagine that it will occasion any serious infringement of any rights you have in any American book. And ere long, doubtless, we shall have something of an international law—so much desired by all American writers—which shall settle this matter upon the basis of justice. The only marvel is, that it does not now exist.

The copies of "Mardi" have ∧ ^not^ yet come to hand, tho' I sent to the Harnden & Co, to inquire.

Yours Sincerely

H Melville.

Richard Bentley Esq
New Burlington Street

69⌉ [RICHARD BENTLEY]. Manuscript profit and loss statement. [London], March 4, 1852. 1 page, 4⅜″ x 7¼″. Published: Birss, ed., "A Mere Sale to Effect," 252–253.

Profit & Loss a/c on publication of Herman Melville's works- to 4 March 1852

			Deficit
Mardi: published ^1849^ March. On joint a/c- Paid author £210			
	deduct total profit realized—		141.12.61
	(final)		
			£68.7.6
Redburn –	do Sept. do—do— Paid author £100 –		
	deduct profit realized—		23.12.6
	(415 copies on hand)		76.7.6
White Jacket	do Jan 1850 – Copy't of 1st Edn purchased		
	for £200—	Deficit to this date.	173.9.6
(629 copies on hand)			
The Whale – published Oct 1851 on joint a/c. Paid author			£150
	(217 copies on hand) deduct profit realized		15, 135—
	Present Deficit		£453.4.6
Less by Value of stock 2740 Vols @ 9—			
	[added in pencil] say		103.4.6
[added in pencil] Probable Eventual Loss			£350

The young Herman Melville spent much of the years 1839–1844 at sea on merchant, whaling, and navy vessels. His experiences in this half-decade gave him the source material for his best-known works, including *Moby-Dick, Typee, Omoo, Redburn, White-Jacket,* and "Billy Budd, Sailor." Melville's first novel, *Typee,* was a partly autobiographical account of his time in the Marquesas Islands after jumping ship from a whaling voyage. Melville developed the narrative from the accounts of his travels with which he regaled his family members and friends, who urged him to turn his experiences into a book.[96]

Melville's elder brother, Gansevoort, acted as agent for the book's publication, making arrangements with Wiley and Putnam in New York and, while in England on a diplomatic appointment, with John Murray in London. The plan was to publish the works simultaneously, to protect it against being pirated. Since there was no international copyright agreement between Britain and the United States, American printers were free to pirate British works and vice versa. An arrangement developed whereby British publishers would issue the works in England a day before their official publication in America, thus securing an enforceable British copyright. *Typee* was one of the first examples of an attempt to secure copyright in both countries through simultaneous publication.[97]

Typee was Melville's greatest success in his lifetime, but was also a scandalous publication. Many of its reviewers were offended by Melville's positive depiction of the Pacific Islanders' "savage" customs and by his critical and satirical presentation of Christian missionary efforts in the region. Among those who took offense at the book was one-half of the book's own publishing partnership: George P. Putnam had agreed to issue the book without consulting his partner, the more conservative John Wiley. Nevertheless, the book found an eager audience in both America and England.

Gansevoort Melville planned to continue in his role as Herman Melville's international agent, but the elder Melville brother died after a sudden and rapidly progressing illness in May 1846. At the end of the year, Melville wrote to his brother's colleague John Brodhead, a colleague of Gansevoort who succeeded him in his diplomatic appointment. In the December 30 letter (plate 11), Melville calmly but

96. Hershel Parker, *Herman Melville: A Biography* (Baltimore: The Johns Hopkins University Press, 1996–2002), v.1:354–355.
97. Ibid., v.1:394–395.

New York Dec 30th 1846

John Romyn Brodhead Esq

Dear Sir:— The long-
standing acquaintance between our
families, and particularly that between
my late brother Mr Gansevoort Melville
and yourself, induce me to solicit
a favor which my own slight acquaintance
with you would not perhaps warrant.
By granting it, as I think you will,
you will confer that which I shall
not forget,

I have recently made an
arrangement with the Harpers to bring
out a new work of mine. But altho'
it has just gone to press, they are to
defer publication until I have
concluded arrangements to bring out the

PLATE 11.
63] Herman Melville. Autograph letter signed to John Brodhead, December
30, 1846, page 1 of 4.

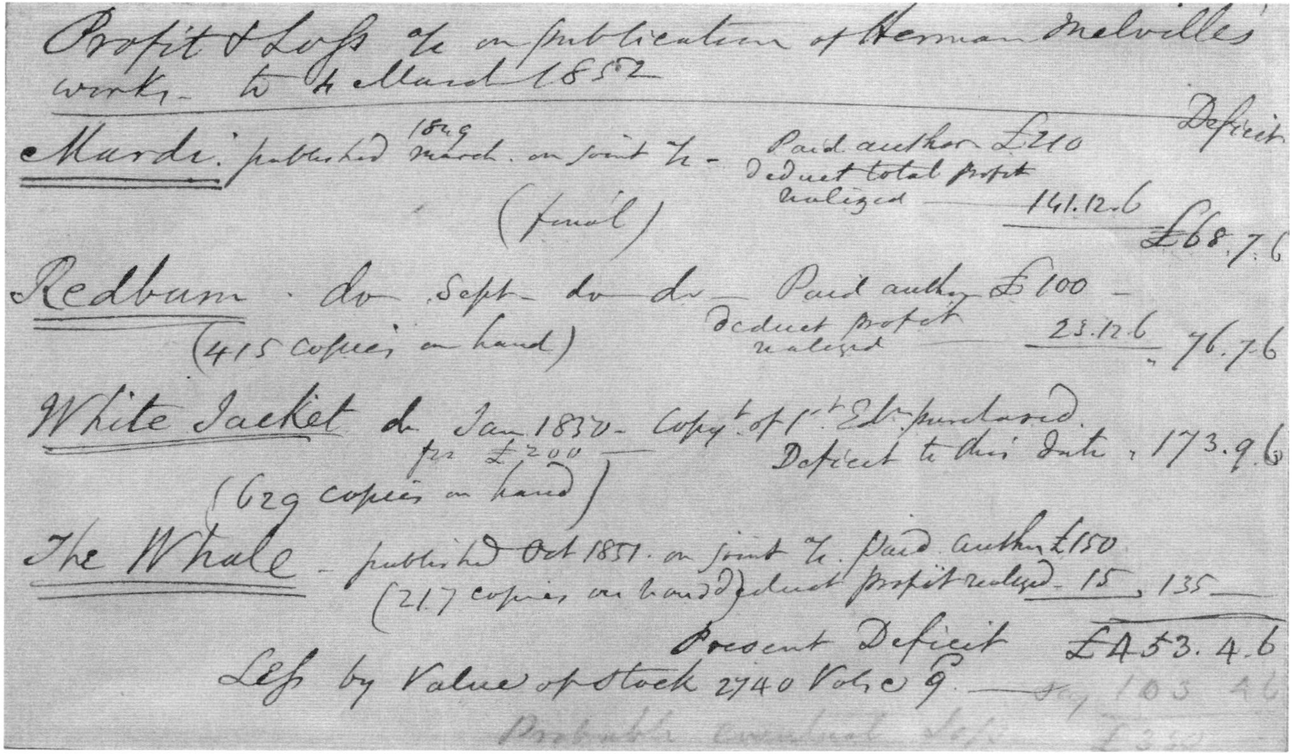

PLATE 12.
69] [Richard Bentley]. Manuscript profit and loss statement for books by Herman Melville.

desperately appeals to Brodhead to do him the favor of completing the book's sale to Murray and delivering the proof sheets prepared by Harper & Bros. to Murray. He emphasizes that the task is simple—"a mere sale to effect"—and that if Brodhead declines it "will occasion me no small pecuniary loss."[98] Brodhead received the letter on January 14, 1847, and immediately agreed to assist Melville.[99]

The path to *Omoo*'s publication was complicated by an erroneous assumption at the customs house. When the novel's proof sheets arrived in London on the steamer *Hibernia*, English customs agents seized them, believing them to be pirated. A draft of Brodhead's letter to the customs house on February 18 quotes the customs report, which declares that the parcel, "on being examined at the Customs, was found to contain an American reprint of an English author, entitled 'a Narrative of a voyage to the north seas; by Melville', —and as such . . . was seized by the Examining officer." Brodhead is perplexed by the situation, and even points out that the customs officers have misidentified the title of the work they have seized (which describes a voyage to the South Seas, not the North). Broadhead seeks to set the record straight: "It is an unpublished, and altogether original American work, and so far from its being a reprint of an English work, by an English Author, it has never been published at all." In the draft's many changes and deletions, we see his struggle to give the correct weight to his anger: in referring to the officer who seized the proofs, he refers to "the superabundance of his zeal," his "great ignorance," and states that he "has most unjustifiably transcended his duty," but deletes a reference to "incompetency" and a vague threat that the officer has "exposed himself to the consequences of his act." In these revisions we can see Brodhead's anger turning into a goal-oriented resolve; his guiding desire is not that the customs agent be punished, but that the parcel be released to him so that it can be published. Brodhead's letter quickly achieved its goal; on

98. Herman Melville, *Correspondence*, ed. Lynn Horth, Northwestern-Newberry ed., The Writings of Herman Melville (the Northwestern-Newberry Edition) 14 (Evanston and Chicago: Northwestern University Press and The Newberry Library, 1993), 70–71.
99. Ibid., 70.

February 20, he sent the proof sheets on to John Murray. (The cover letter to Murray makes no mention of the customs seizure.)

Murray was pleased with the novel, and wrote to Brodhead on February 26 to offer £150 for the right to publish it in England, on the understanding that it would not appear in America before his edition was released. This was a significant sum, even taking into account the cost of transferring it overseas—particularly so when even successful American authors of the era were often obligated to pay for the printing of their own work in their own country. Brodhead successfully negotiated for payment immediately upon publication, and Murray, in a letter of March 1, agreed to make an up-front payment of a slightly lesser fee (£144.3.4). Of this sum, Melville took only £140, leaving Brodhead the balance.[100]

Brodhead continued to serve as Melville's literary agent on his next book, *Mardi*, in 1849. But John Murray, disappointed in the sales of *Omoo* and at Melville's increasing preference for fiction over unembellished travel narratives, declined it. Brodhead instead sold the manuscript to another London publisher, Richard Bentley, who offered Melville a generous advance of £210.[101] *Mardi* was negatively reviewed in England, and Melville and Bentley corresponded in June and July regarding its reception, the lack of an international copyright agreement between England and America, and the terms for the publication of Melville's next book, *Redburn*. In a letter to Bentley on June 5, 1849, Melville reassured the publisher that Mardi "will reach those for whom it is intended ... 'Mardi', in its higher purposes, has not been written in vain."[102] His next book, he assured Bentley, would be "a plain, straightforward, amusing narrative of personal experience — the son of a gentleman on his first voyage to sea as a sailor — no metaphysics, no conic-sections, nothing but cakes & ale." [103]

---

100. Parker, *Herman Melville*, v.1:483; John H. Birss, ed., "'A Mere Sale to Effect' with Letters of Herman Melville," *New Colophon* 1, no. part 3 (July 1948): 244.
101. Parker, *Herman Melville*, v.1:619.
102. Melville, letter to Richard Bentley, June 5, 1849. In Melville, *Correspondence*, 131–32.
103. Ibid., 132.

Bentley wrote a generally discouraging response on June 20. He commented that *Mardi* was not as satisfying a read as *Typee* and *Omoo* had been. Moreover, a recent court decision in England declared that American works were not covered by English copyright, meaning publishers like himself were exposed to greater risk of having their books pirated. He offered a more modest advance of £100 for *Redburn,* noting: "surrounded as I am with the want of success of Mardi and the stupid decision, at present with regard to copyright, [a greater advance] will not be in my power to give."[104]

In his response on July 20, Melville accepted Bentley's terms, and offered optimistic words on the future sales of *Mardi*: "there are goodly harvests which ripen late, especially when the grain is remarkably strong . . . I need not assure you how deeply I regret that, for any period, you should find this venture of 'Mardi' an unprofitable thing for you; & I should feel still more grieved, did I suppose it was going to eventuate in a positive loss to you. But this cannot be in the end."[105] Unfortunately, Melville's optimism regarding the English sales of his works was not borne out. He received generous advances for each of the four books he published with Richard Bentley (*Mardi, Redburn, White-Jacket,* and *Moby-Dick*), but none sold well enough to prove profitable for their publisher.

When Melville offered Bentley the novel *Pierre* in early 1852, the publisher reviewed his accounts to determine the state of his deficit for Melville's books. A manuscript memorandum (plate 12) shows his calculations: In its first year of publication Bentley had made less than £17 on *White-Jacket,* for which Melville had received £200; even the "straightforward, amusing narrative," *Redburn,* for which Bentley had paid a more modest advance of £100, had earned back less than a quarter of that sum. Calculating the value of his remaining stock of Melville's books, he estimated a net loss of £350 for the four books. Bentley wrote to Melville on March 4, providing him with a summary of the accounts and offering some advice:

---

104. Richard Bentley, letter to Herman Melville, June 20, 1849. In ibid., 596.
105. Melville, letter to Richard Bentley, July 20, 1849. In ibid., 133; also Birss, "'A Mere Sale to Effect' with Letters of Herman Melville," 247.

"Your books, I fear, are produced in too rapid succession. It was not long ago since The Whale was published—not time sufficient has yet been given to it, before another is ready!"[106] Nevertheless, he offered to share the costs and eventual profits of publishing *Pierre* with the author—but without an advance.

Melville's response, sent on April 16, "was a long, maundering, specious, self-justifying, begging, try-anything letter."[107] He entreated Bentley to forget his losses on the past publications: "let bygones be bygones; let those previous books, for the present, take care of themselves. For here now we have a *new book*, and what shall we say about *this?* If nothing has been made on the old books, may not something be made out of the new?"[108] After requesting an advance of £100, Melville concludes with a final postscript suggesting that the book could be published anonymously. Needless to say, Bentley was not convinced, and his publishing relationship with Melville was concluded.

70⎤ HERMAN MELVILLE. Autograph letter signed to James Billson. New York, September 5, 1885. 3 pages. Published: Melville, *Correspondence*, 488–489.

New York
Sept. 5, '85

Dear Sir:

I have to thank you for two papers received some months ago, one containing an article by your hand on the poet Thomson, the other referring to the South Sea Islands (and was this too written by yourself?) Both interesting to me: the first because my interest in the author of the "City of Dreadful Night" was measurably awakened by it.

Moreover, I must thank you for your note of Oct. 18th Believe me, its friendly proffer of good offices, should occasion occur, this I was, and remain, grateful for.

106. Richard Bentley, letter to Herman Melville, March 4, 1852. In Melville, *Correspondence*, 618.
107. Parker, *Herman Melville*, v.2:106.
108. Melville, letter to Richard Bentley, April 16, 1852. In Melville, *Correspondence*, 226–27.

But yet further to bring up arrears, my acknowledgments are due for a copy of "The Academy" received the other day containing a poem of Robert Buchanan "Socrates in Camden." Far more than any reason, the Piece could not but give me pleasure. Aside from its poetic quality, that is implyed in it the fact, that the writer has intuitively penetrated beneath the surface of certain matters here. It is the insight of genius and the fresh mind. The tribute to Walt Whitman has the ring of strong sincerity. As to the incidental allusion to my humble self, it is overpraise, to be sure; but I can't help that, tho' I am alive to the spirit that dictated it.

But a letter on almost any theme, is but an inadequate vehicle, so I must say no more.

> With good wishes ~~to~~ for you
> Very truly
> Herman Melville

Mr James Billson

Melville's literary fortunes declined after the commercial failure of his novels in the 1850s. He ceased writing novels after the publication of *The Confidence-Man: His Masquerade* in 1857. In 1866, he was appointed as a customs inspector in New York, where he remained until his retirement at the end of 1885. In the final decades of his life, he published only two volumes of poetry, neither of which sold well. In one letter, Melville referred to *Clarel*, the last of his works to be published in his lifetime, as "eminently adapted for unpopularity."[109] Though *Typee* had been a success, he was largely forgotten as an author in the latter half of the century.

In 1884 James Billson, an English admirer of Melville's writings, began a correspondence with the author that continued throughout the final years of Melville's life. Billson frequently sent books and magazines to Melville. In September 1885, he sent along a copy of the London *Academy* containing Robert Buchanan's poem "Socrates in Camden, With a Look Round." In this poem, the Scottish poet recounts a meeting with Walt Whitman, whom he lauds. Buchanan contrasts Whitman with popular poets of the day, whom he mocks in an extended metaphoric passage as "haberdashers." One author who merits comparison with Whitman, in Buchanan's estimation, is Melville:

---

109. Quoted in Parker, *Herman Melville*, v.2:863.

While Melville, sea-compelling man,
Before whose wand Leviathan
Rose hoary white upon the Deep,
With awful sounds that stirred its sleep,
Melville, whose magic drew Typee,
Radiant as Venus, from the sea,
Sits all forgotten or ignored,
While haberdashers are adored![110]

The passage on Melville—which continues with further poetic praise of *Typee* and *Moby Dick*—was deleted for its inclusion in Buchanan's 1898 book *The New Rome*, appearing only in its original publication in the *Academy*.

The original version implies that Melville was not, in fact, so well known in England: the first mention of his name is accompanied with a footnote regarding his obscurity: "Hermann Melville, author of *Typee, The White Whale*, &c. I sought everywhere for this Triton, who is still living somewhere in New York. No one seemed to know anything of the one great imaginative writer fit to stand shoulder to shoulder with Whitman on that continent."[111] Parker remarks that Buchanan's inability to locate Melville was surprising: the author was listed in the city directory, and during his trip to America he visited several others who were acquainted with Melville.[112] Nevertheless, Buchanan did not expect his readers to know the author to whom he referred; several other authors are mentioned by name in the poem with no such clarifying identification.

Melville replied to Billson on September 5, 1885, with an acknowledgement of the poem's praise: "For more than one reason, this Piece could not but give me pleasure. Aside from its poetic quality, there is implied in it the fact, that the writer has intuitively penetrated beneath the surface of certain matters here. It is the insight of genius and the fresh mind." He mentions Whitman by name, though he does little to elaborate on his own feelings about

110. Robert Williams Buchanan, "The New Rome 1898," *Robert Buchanan (1841-1901)*, 2006, http://www.robertbuchanan.co.uk/html/rome9.html (accessed May 8, 2017).
111. Ibid.
112. Parker, *Herman Melville*, v. 2:873.

his fellow author: "The tribute to Walt Whitman has the ring of strong sincerity." He concludes his comments with humility: "As to the incidental allusion to my humble self, it is overpraise, to be sure; but I can't help that, tho' I am alive to the spirit that dictated it."[113] The letter shows Melville, some three decades after he effectively exited the literary world, remaining interested in but somewhat detached from it.

113. Melville, letter to James Billson, September 5, 1885. In Melville, *Correspondence*, 489.

A Carol of Harvest, for 1867.

By Walt Whitman.

1

¹A song of the grass and fields !
A song of the soil, & the good
        green grass !
A song no more of the city streets;
A song of the soil of fields.

²A song with the smell of sun-
        dried hay, where the nimble
        pitchers handle the pitch-fork;
A song tasting of new wheat, and
        of fresh-husk'd maize.

2

³For the lands, & for these passionate
        days, & for myself,

72] Walt Whitman. Autograph manuscript poem, "A Carol of Harvest, for 1867," page 1 of 18.

Walt Whitman: Process and Presentation

71⟧ Walt Whitman. Autograph manuscript fragments from "By Blue Ontario's Shore." [Washington, ca. 1867]. Four leaves consisting of several pieced-together fragments, 8⅛″ x 5″, 4¼″ x 7½″, 4⅞″ x 7⅞″, and 9″ x 7¾″.

72⟧ Walt Whitman. Autograph manuscript poem, "A Carol of Harvest, for 1867." [Washington, ca. August 1867]. 18 numbered leaves of blue-lined notebook paper, 9½″ x 7¾″.

This pair of poetry manuscripts illustrates Whitman's writing process. Alice Birney notes that Whitman "habitually scribbled on odd scraps of paper, on backs of poetry drafts or envelopes. He kept perhaps hundreds of handmade notebooks . . . his proofs often bear important holographic corrections, and unique issues of his books might include bound-in manuscript pages or printing plates left over from other editions."[114] In short, much like Emily Dickinson (who wrote her poems in scrapbooks containing pasted-in material and ephemera), Whitman's manuscript habits were complex, and often involved combining pieces and scraps from multiple sources. Moreover, the line between Whitman's prose and his poetry is a blurry one, and in his journals he would often move from prose to verse and back again.

The present manuscript fragments from the poem "By Blue Ontario's Shore" (plate 13) illustrate Whitman's writing habits. The poem itself is a hybrid work, having grown out of the prose preface

114. Alice L. Birney, "Collectors and Collections, Whitman," ed. J. R. LeMaster and Donald D. Kummings, *Walt Whitman: An Encyclopedia* (New York: Routledge, 1998), 136.

to the 1855 first edition of *Leaves of Grass*. It first appeared as a poem in the 1856 second edition, under the title "The Poem of Many in One." Whitman continued to revise and alter the poem over the years, most significantly in the aftermath of the Civil War. In these manuscript fragments, we see Whitman's process of assembling poetry piece-by-piece, pasting together scraps of paper with individual lines; rethinking and rewriting words, phrases, and lines; and revising penciled draft with ink. These fragments show the *work* of his poetry, the embodied experience of constructing a poem. Whitman's process often extended from pencil, pen, and paste directly to the printing press: he was intimately involved in not just the publication but the physical production of many of his books, even going so far as to set the type on several of his own works.[115]

The manuscript for "A Carol of Harvest" is a far more formal affair. Rather than a working draft, this is a fair copy, most likely the manuscript of the poem Whitman submitted for publication in the *Galaxy* in 1867.[116] W. C. Church, the magazine's editor, had commissioned Whitman (through their mutual acquaintance William Douglas O'Connor) to write the poem: "It seems to me that this glorious harvest of 1867, sown & reaped by the returned soldiers, ought to be sung in verse . . . Walt Whitman is the man to chaunt the song."[117]

Whitman sent this manuscript to Church on August 7, 1867, with a cover letter that shows the care Whitman took regarding the appearance of his work in print: "I wish, if acceptable, you would have it set up *immediately*, proved, read carefully by copy, carefully corrected, & then a *good proof* taken & sent to me here . . . If practicable, I should like to have the piece commence on an odd-numbered

115. Ed Folsom, *Walt Whitman: Whitman Making Books, Books Making Whitman: A Catalog & Commentary* (Iowa City, Iowa: Obermann Center for Advanced Studies, University of Iowa, 2005), http://whitmanarchive.org/criticism/current/anc.00150.html (accessed May 8, 2017).

116. In his publication of a draft manuscript of the poem, Bowers expresses certainty of the existence of this manuscript, though he had not seen it. See Fredson Bowers, "The Manuscript of Walt Whitman's 'A Carol of Harvest, for 1867,'" *Modern Philology* 52, no. 1 (1954): 30.

117. W. C. Church, letter to William O'Connor, August 1, 1867. Quoted in Walt Whitman, *The Correspondence, Volume I: 1842–1867*, ed. Edwin Haviland Miller (New York: New York University Press, 1961), 336.

page of the magazine—& wish it could come the second article in the Number."[118] He wrote to Church four days later, concerned that he had not received the requested proof.[119] The manuscript includes added notes to the printer in blue pencil indicating the author's preference for typefaces and indentations: "These figures in Long Primer . . . indent 4 ems." The poem appeared in the September 1867 issue, but the printers do not seem to have followed all of Whitman's instructions: the line indentations in this publication were three ems rather than four, and it was not the second item in the issue, but the seventh.

73⌉ WALT WHITMAN. *Memoranda During the War.* Camden, New Jersey: Author's Publication, 1875-'76. Original red cloth. Inscribed by the author on the remembrance leaf: "[To] Joseph C Baldwin / [From] his friend the Author."

74⌉ [WALT WHITMAN.] "Remembrance Copy." [Camden, New Jersey: the Author, 1875]. Unbound proof of the remembrance leaf bound into copies of *Memoranda During the War.*
Whitman worked as a volunteer nurse during the Civil War, and the experience made a lasting impact on the poet. Shortly after this experience, he was inspired by Louisa May Alcott's publication of *Hospital Sketches* to compose a memoir of his own war experiences. Though he anticipated strong sales to hospitals and veterans, his initial proposal to abolitionist publisher James Redpath in 1863 failed to lead to an immediate publication.[120] It was over a decade before the book was actually published.

Whitman had 1,000 copies of *Memoranda During the War* printed in 1875, and by the following spring had bound 750 of them in-

118. Ibid. (Letter 242).
119. Ibid. (Letter 243).
120. Roy Morris, Jr., *The Better Angel: Walt Whitman in the Civil War* (Oxford & New York: Oxford University Press, 2000), 146.

dividually and incorporated another 100 into the "Centennial Edition" of *Two Rivulets*.[121] The separately bound copies of *Memoranda . . .* included a "remembrance leaf" on which the author personally inscribed each copy to its recipient or purchaser. The remembrance leaf formalizes personalization: the inscriptions render each copy unique and personal, but the form-letter style of the biographical sketch on the leaf seems to diminish that uniqueness. The present copy is inscribed to James C. Baldwin, a young man from Philadelphia who moved to Elliotstown, Illinois in the mid-1870s and worked there as a sharecropper. According to Charley Shively, Whitman and Baldwin were lovers. Before his departure for Illinois, Baldwin received a ring from the poet; Whitman later loaned Baldwin money when his farm yielded a disappointing corn crop.[122]

121. Wells & Goldsmith state that "it is improbable that more than a hundred copies were issued," but Folsom indicates that 750 copies were bound with the remembrance leaf. See Carolyn Wells and Alfred F. Goldsmith, *A Concise Bibliography of the Works of Walt Whitman, with a Supplement of Fifty Books about Whitman* (Boston: Houghton Mifflin, 1922), 19–20; Folsom, *Walt Whitman*.
122. See Charley Shively, ed., *Calamus Lovers: Walt Whitman's Working Class Camerados* (San Francisco: Gay Sunshine Press, 1987), 124–26, 132–35.

CHAPTER EIGHT
"Friend Bliss": Mark Twain and His Publishers

═══

75⎤ MARK TWAIN. *The Innocents Abroad* [prospectus]. [Hartford: The American Publishing Company, 1869]. With hand-made wooden presentation box, engraved on cover: "Mark, Twain."

Most of Mark Twain's books were published by the largest and most successful subscription publishing house of his day: Elisha Bliss's American Publishing Company. This was an undistinguished corner of publishing at the time: Clemens himself commented that "Mighty few books that come strictly under the head of *literature* will sell by subscription."[123] Typical subscription books dealt with matters of current events, autobiography, religion, or travel, and were typically housed within attractive, occasionally gaudy, and often cheaply produced bindings. Clemens's first book for Bliss, *The Innocents Abroad, or, The New Pilgrims' Progress*, narrates a voyage to Europe and the Holy Land.

This and Twain's other books for the American Publishing Company were sold door-to-door by salesman in advance of publication. To help make sales, subscription houses would prepare a prospectus containing selected materials from the book, examples of the various bindings available, and sales blanks for the salesman to make a record of copies sold. According to Twain scholar Hamlin Hill, the selections included in the prospectus for *Innocents Abroad* are "Mark Twain at his most raucously anti-intellectual. The appeal, in other words, was to the popular reader, and Bliss calculated with

---

123. Quoted in Hamlin Hill, *Mark Twain and Elisha Bliss* (Columbia, Mo.: University of Missouri Press, 1964), 11.

great perception that the average man would rather have his guide-book laced with humor and iconoclasm than with piety and a sermon."[124] Bliss's approach paid off, and *Innocents Abroad* sold over 77,000 copies in its first sixteen months—a number unmatched by any other book by Mark Twain in his lifetime.[125]

The wooden case accompanying the present prospectus, with Twain's name wood-burned into the upper cover, is thought to have been handmade by the salesman, William Aldrich of Wisconsin.

76] SAMUEL L. CLEMENS. Autograph letter signed ("Mark") to Elisha Bliss. Elmira, New York, May 20, [1870]. 1 page. 7⅞" x 5". Published: Victor Fischer and Michael B. Frank, eds. *Mark Twain's Letters, Volume 4: 1870–1871* (Berkeley: University of California Press, 1995), p. 131–132.

> Confidential.
>
> Buf. May 20.
>
> Friend Bliss—
>
> Appleton wants me to furnish a few lines of letter press for a humorous picture-book—that is, two lines of remarks under each picture. I have intimated that if the pictures & the pay are both good, I will do it. What do you think of it? I thought that inasmuch as half the public would think I made the engravings as well as did the letter-press, it would be a unique & splendid advertisements-wherewith to boost the "Innocents." I am to see proofs of the pictures before I contract.
>
> Yrs
>
> Mark.

77] SAMUEL L. CLEMENS. Autograph letter signed ("Mark") to Elisha Bliss. Elmira, New York, July 4, 1870. 3 pages on a single folded leaf, 8¼" x 10¼". Published in *Mark Twain's Letters, Volume 4: 1870–1871*, p. 161–162.

---

124. Hill, *Mark Twain and Elisha Bliss*, p. 37.
125. Hill, *Mark Twain and Elisha Bliss*, p. 39.

Elmira, July 4.

Friend Bliss:

Mr. Langdon is ever so much better, & we have every reason to believe that he is going to get well, & that speedily.

I fancy the book you speak of must be the Appleton book. I cannot think of any other, & have no knowledge of any other. But I shall probably never have to do the Appleton book. They asked me to name a price. I named a pretty stiff one. And at the same time, I said that if it were a subscription book I could afford easier terms. They misunderstood me and thought that I was suggesting that it be made a subscription book — & so they accepted the idea my suggestion and offered higher pay than I spoke of. But I wrote them immediately that they had misconstrued me, & that I could not do a subscription book for them at any price whatever. And moreover, that I could do nothing more than the original proposition called for. And that I could not even do that unless I could do it either before or immediately after my Adirondack trip. They have had two or ample time to have written me half a dozen times since, & haven't done it. Therefore it is far from likely that any "humorous book" is will issue from my pen shortly.

If Mr. L. gets thoroughly well, in time, my wife & I will go straight from Buffalo to Vergennes, VT. the at the end of July, & be joined there by the Twichells. It is our shortest & straightest route to the woods.

We shall be here 10 days or 2 weeks yet. Come — come either here or to Buf.

Yrs

Mark.

78] SAMUEL L. CLEMENS. Autograph letter signed ("Clemens") to Elisha Bliss. Buffalo, New York, October 26, [1870]. 2 pages on a single leaf. 7¾" x 5". Published in Fischer & Frank, eds., *Mark Twain's Letters, Volume 4: 1870–1871*, p. 212–213.

Buf. Oct. 26.

Friend Bliss:

My man took my telegram down town asking for answer to my letter, & then brought your letter up from my office.

It is all right. It is too late now to get out the annual. If I believed that writing for the Galaxy hurt the sale of my books without anybody who didn't make that excuse simply because they wanted an excuse of some kind, I would retire from the magazine tomorrow. But I cannot believe it. It is a good advertisement for me—as you show when you desire me to quit the Galaxy & go on your paper. But if I am hurting myself through the Galaxy, I want to know it—& then I will draw out of that & write for no periodical—for ~~certainly~~ I have chewed & drank & sworn, habitually, & have discarded them all, & am well aware that a bad thing should be killed entirely—tapering off is a foolish & dangerous business.

   A week or ten days ago I notified the Galaxy that my year would end with the April number, & although I hated to quit I might find it necessary, because the magazine interfered so much with other work & I half expected to lecture a little next year. I enclose the answer, just received.

[Added in left margin of p. 2:]

Tell Frank to be prompt with his ac/ — my expenses have been as $600 & $700 a month, latterly, because of sickness & funerals, & I don't allow my wife to help pay my bills.
                    Yrs
                    Clemens

79⎤ SAMUEL L. CLEMENS. Autograph letter signed ("S.L. Clemens" and "Clemens") to Elisha Bliss. Buffalo, New York, December 2, [1870]. 3 pages. 7¾″ x 5″. Published in Fischer & Frank, eds., *Mark Twain's Letters, Volume 4: 1870–1871*, p. 256–258.

{Copy}
Don't overlook the Post ~~S.~~ Scripts.
Buf. Dec. 2.
Friend Bliss:
   I'll tell you what I'll do. I'll not take advantage of your ~~perm~~ consent to pay me 10 per cent, but I'll do this. You're to pay me 8½ per cent, & advance me ~~three tho~~ another thousand dollars (in addition to the fifteen hundred,) any time I demand it during 1871, this thousand also to come out of my first earnings on the African book.
∧ ^OVER And further:
   If my man don't get back & I can't write the African book for you, I'll write you a 600 page 8vo. book in place of it, which you are to pay me 8½ per cent copy right on & you to subtract all that $1500 or $2500 from my first receipts on that book.
   How's that?
   1. Don't you see? You get a book, in any event.

⎡ 116 ⎤

2. You pay 8½ pcent. copy right in any event.

3. I ~~lose~~ alone risk that advance-money on my man. If nothing comes of it, I lose it all, you none of it.

~~That extra~~

I would not publish a book through you (or any other person) at a copyright which I believed would preclude your getting your fair & full share of the profits of the enterprise.

Write or telegraph.

Yrs. S.L. Clemens.

[Added in margin of p. 2:]

P.S. Keep this whole thing a dead secret—else we'll have somebody standing ready to launch a book right on our big tidal wave & swim it into a success when it would otherwise fall still-born.

[Added in margin of p.1:]

P.P.S. If this suits, ~~preserve~~ draw a written contract, or else take proper measures to make this fully & legally binding on both of us in its present form. Clemens.

[Added on verso of p. 1:]

{I have been looking into the matter, & my man might need more than the $1500, though I'll not demand the extra $1,000 from you unless he demands it of me, by & bye.}

80┐ SAMUEL L. CLEMENS. Autograph letter signed ("Clemens" and "Mark") to Elisha Bliss. Buffalo, New York, December 20, [1870]. 4 pages. 7¾″ x 5″. Published in Fischer & Frank, eds., *Mark Twain's Letters, Volume 4: 1870–1871*, p. 276–278.

Buf. Dec. 20.

Friend Bliss —

Have just read over, approved & signed that contract, & it will go to you to-night.

Riley is my man—did I introduce him to you in New York? He sails Jan. 4 for Africa. Just read about him in my Galaxy Memoranda for a month or two ago[.] I have forgotten which month, but it is headed "Riley—Newspaper respondent." Riley is perfectly honorable & reliable in every possible way—his simple promise is as good as any man's oath. I have roomed with him long, & have known him years. He has "roughed it" ∧ in many savage countries & is as tough as a pine-knot. He is the very best man in the entire United States for this mission—& when he comes back & tells me his story in my study (for he is a splendid talker,)

I'll set it down red hot, & that book will just make the "Innocents" sick! He is to talk to me 2 hours a day, ~~till I have~~ week after week & month after month till I have pumped him entirely dry. I boarding him free in my house & paying $50 a month besides. I'll get two 600-page books out of his experiences, see if I don't. And if you make the first one go, we won't have any trouble about who shall publish the second one. I mean to keep Riley traveling for me till I wear him out!

All this is "mum."

Yrs Clemens.

P.S. When I tel[e]graphed you to send the check for $1,500 it didn't occur to me that maybe you'd rather have the contract signed first, but that was just like-l my thoughtlessness. But send the check to me on New York made payable to the order of J.H. Riley, & I will forward it to him at Washington, as he desired me to do. If you haven't sent it yet, you may make it in two drafts, one for $100— and one for $1,400.—

How is my brother getting along, & what sort of a home has he gone into?

Mark

In the years immediately following the publication of *Innocents Abroad,* Twain and Bliss were both eager to recreate its runaway success. At the same time, the relationship between the author and his publisher was a difficult one. Though Clemens generally greeted his publisher in letters with "Friend Bliss," their relationship was fraught, filled with distrust and mutual manipulation. In private, Clemens referred to Bliss as "the old fox," and he attacked him viciously in his autobiography:

I never heard him tell the truth, so far as I can remember. He was a most repulsive creature. When he was after dollars he showed the intense earnestness and eagerness of a circular-saw. In a small, mean, peanut-stand fashion, he was sharp and shrewd. But above that level he was destitute of intelligence; his brain was a loblolly, and he had the gibbering laugh of an idiot. It is my belief that Bliss never did an honest thing in his life, when he had a chance to do a dishonest one. I have had contact with several conspicuously mean men, but they were noble compared to this bastard monkey.[126]

126. Mark Twain, *Autobiography of Mark Twain, Volume 1*, ed. Harriet Elinor Smith, Reader's edition (Berkeley: University of California Press, 2012), 243.

The roots of Clemens's anger toward Bliss lie in the events of 1870. Clemens was frustrated that Bliss had delayed the publication of *Innocents Abroad*, which he had originally delivered to Bliss in 1868 and hoped would be released that year. The contract for the book, signed on October 28, called for a release in spring 1869, but the book did not actually appear until August. Clemens was angry with Bliss over the delay, but his irritation was eased somewhat by the success of the book.[127]

Innocents Abroad led to a demand for more work by Mark Twain, and the correspondence between Clemens and Bliss shows both men maneuvering for the ideal position. Clemens made Bliss aware of offers he had received from other publishers. He received and accepted an offer to write a humorous column for the *Galaxy,* and communicated the terms of the offer to Bliss in a letter of March 11; it appears that Bliss tried to dissuade Clemens from taking on this position.[128] Clemens also received offers from book publishers; on May 20, he informed Bliss of an offer from Appleton and Co. "to furnish a few lines of letter press for a humorous picture-book—that is, two lines of remarks under each picture. I have intimated that if the pictures & the pay are both good, I will do it." He presents the proposed volume as "a unique & splendid advertisement" for *Innocents Abroad,* but the implication is clear; Clemens wanted Bliss to know that other publishers were interested, and might be willing to pay him well for his work. Clemens wrote again to Bliss on July 4 concerning the Appleton offer, explaining that he had turned them down, implying that doing a subscription book for another house would conflict with the American Publishing Co., but he was also careful to hint that he could have received very favorable terms from Appleton: "They asked me to name a price. I named a pretty stiff one."

For his part, Bliss endeavored to obtain commitments from Clemens, and they entered into contracts for two additional books in

127. Hamlin Hill, "Mark Twain's Quarrels with Elisha Bliss," *American Literature* 33, no. 4 (1962): 444–45, doi:10.2307/2922611.
128. Mark Twain, letter to Elisha Bliss, March 11, 1870. In Mark Twain, *Mark Twain's Letters, Volume 4: 1870-1871,* ed. Victor Fischer and Michael B. Frank, The Mark Twain Papers (Berkeley: University of California Press, 1995), 90–91.

1870. Bliss also hired Clemens's brother Orion to work on *The American Publisher*, a magazine that served primarily to advertise the company's subscription volumes. Clemens believed that Orion's employment was intended as a means to further entangle Twain with the American Publishing Co.[129] It ultimately took Twain nearly a decade to extricate himself from the contracts he and Bliss signed in 1870.

The first of these new contracts was for another humorous travel book, *Roughing It*, this one describing Clemens's journeys in the American West. Bliss granted Twain a 7.5% royalty on the book, an increase above the 5% he received for *Innocents Abroad*, but lower than what he claimed he had been offered by Appleton.[130] Clemens soon began work on the new book, and had high hopes for it to outsell *Innocents*. He withdrew from his position at the *Galaxy* to work on the manuscript, but made sure to explain to Bliss that it was his own decision, and not the result of Bliss's requests. In a letter of October 26, he writes:

> If I believed that writing for the Galaxy hurt the sale of my books . . . I would retire from the magazine to-morrow. But I cannot believe it. It is a good advertisement for me—as you show when you desire me to quit the Galaxy & go on your paper. But if I *am* hurting myself through the Galaxy, I want to know it—& then I will draw out of that & write for *no* periodical—for I have chewed & drank & sworn, habitually, & have discarded them all, & am well aware that a bad thing should be killed entirely—*tapering off* is a foolish & dangerous business.

Only after this lengthy explanation does he inform Bliss that he has, in fact, retired from the *Galaxy*, lest it interfere with his other work.

The second contract Clemens and Bliss signed in 1870 was for an ill-fated project. The idea was for another travel book, this one on South Africa, and in particular on the South African diamond rush. Clemens concocted a plan to send his friend James H. Riley to Africa to research the book and take voluminous notes, at the same time prospecting for diamonds, the profits from which he would share with Clemens. Clemens would then write a book from

129. Hill, "Mark Twain's Quarrels with Elisha Bliss," 445.
130. Mark Twain, letter to Elisha Bliss, August 2, 1870. In Mark Twain, *Mark Twain's Letters, Volume 4: 1870–1871*, 179–80.

the notes as if he himself had gone on the trip, the result to be published by the American Publishing Co.[131] In a letter of December
2, Twain laid out the plan, which also called for an increase of his
royalty share to 8.5% and an advance of $1,500 (later increased to
$2,000) to cover Riley's travel expenses. Naturally, Clemens did not
mention his side-deal with Riley regarding diamond profits. In a
letter to Bliss on December 20, Clemens spoke highly of Riley, and
expressed excitement about the collaboration. Unfortunately, Clemens's stated intention to "keep Riley traveling . . . till I wear him out"
proved disturbingly prescient. Riley spent three months in South
Africa, failing to find a single precious stone. On his return trip, with
a mere nineteen pages of notes, he contracted blood poisoning and
died. The diamond mine book never materialized, and Twain forgot
about the contract.

81⌉ SAMUEL L. CLEMENS. Autograph manuscript
table of contents for *Mark Twain's Sketches, New and
Old*. [N.p., ca. 1871–1875]. 9 pages, 8″ x 5″.

In 1870 Clemens conceived of a collection of his humorous
sketches, and as early as January 1871, he told Elisha Bliss
that the work was nearly ready for publication. "Name the
Sketch book '*Mark Twain's Sketches*' & go on canvassing like
mad . . . In the course of a week I can have most of the matter ready for you I think. Am working like sin on it."[132] He
and Bliss soon thought better of the timing of the volume, and
put the project on hold. It ultimately appeared under the title
Mark Twain's Sketches, New and Old in 1875. This working
manuscript of the contents of the collection (plate 14) differs
in several major respects from the published version. In addition to the order of many pieces being different, the draft
includes twenty additional sketches than what was ultimately
published. A note next to one sketch, "The Undertaker's Chat,"

131. Hill, *Mark Twain and Elisha Bliss*, p. 129–30.
132. Mark Twain, letter to Elisha Bliss, January 3, 1871. In Mark Twain, *Mark
Twain's Letters, Volume 4: 1870–1871*, 295. (Unrelated deletion by Twain
omitted).

asks, "Where is this?" The manuscript gives valuable insight into Clemens's editorial process in assembling materials for the editor with whom he published his most famous works.

82] SAMUEL L. CLEMENS. Autograph letter signed ("S L C") to Frank Bliss. Heidelberg, July 13, [1878]. 4 pages on 2 folded leaves. 7¾" x 5". Published: Hamlin Hill, ed. *Mark Twain's Letters to His Publishers, 1867–1894* (Berkeley and Los Angeles: University of California Press, 1967), p. 107–108.

Heidelberg, July 13

Dear Frank —

Yours of June 28ᵗʰ arrived last night, making the trip in the usual time, 14 days. If I were to send you the power of attorney now, you would receive it July 27—ten days too late. I am very sorry you didn't start it a couple of weeks earlier. I hope things went satisfactorily & that your father remains in his place. I should have voted for him, of course.

As I wrote you, a week or so ago, I am making fair progress, but of course it isn't <u>great</u> progress, because it costs me more days to <u>get</u> material than to write it up. I have written 400 pages of MS—that is to say, 4,000 about ∧ ⁴⁵ ᵒʳ 50,000 words, or one-fourth of a book, but it is in disconnected form & cannot be used ᵂ until joined together by the writing of at least a dozen intermediate chapters. These intermediate chapters cannot be rightly written until we are settled down for the fall & winter in Munich.

I have been gathering a lot of excellent matter here during the past ten days (stuff which has never been in a book) & shall finish gathering it in a week more. Then we shall leave, & be on the wing for 2 months, during which time I shall not be able to write more than 200 ~~or possibly 300~~ pages, perhaps. Can't tell, yet. I shall be mostly on foot, with Twichell, the first 5 or 6 weeks, & shall write up in full every night if not too tired.

If you should need to write me in the meantime, direct to Heidelberg, care Koester & Co, Bankers, & I will ask them to forward it.

Yr truly
SLC.

83] SAMUEL L. CLEMENS. Autograph manuscript, *A Tramp Abroad,* chapter 42: "Switzerland." [Paris, ca. May 15–May 25, 1879]. 38 pages, bound with the printed version of the chapter. 7⅞" x 4⅞".

84⌉ MARK TWAIN. *A Tramp Abroad.* Hartford: American Publishing Company, 1880. First edition in original red cloth. A pencil note indicates this copy is from the library of Frank Bliss.

In 1878, Clemens signed a secret contract with Elisha Bliss's son, Frank, who was preparing to resign his position at the American Publishing Co. to start his own subscription house. He then left for Europe to begin work on *A Tramp Abroad,* a travel book on central and southern Europe.

Clemens worked on the book throughout 1878 and into 1879. A letter to Frank Bliss on July 13, 1878 indicates that the work got off to a slow start. By mid-July, about a quarter of the book was finished, but only "in disconnected form." Work was proceeding faster in the spring of 1879, and according to Hamlin Hill, Clemens completed nine chapters of the book between May 15 and 25, including chapter 42, on Switzerland.

Elisha Bliss angled to get Twain's next book for his own publishing house, unaware he was competing with his own son. In February 1879, nearly a decade after the contract for the diamond prospecting book was signed, Elisha Bliss informed Clemens that he considered that contract unfulfilled, even though the American Publishing Co. had issued other books without contract since that date: "You have never intimated to me that you considered 'Gilded Age' The Sketches, or Tom Sawyer as being the book to take the place of the Riley book, consequently the $2000 has never been deducted from the copyright but has stood against you." Twain capitulated, finally agreeing to publish *A Tramp Abroad* with the American Publishing Co., albeit with the favorable provision that the company canvass for no other titles for nine months after its publication. The Francis E. Bliss Company issued only a single book—Buffalo Bill Cody's autobiography—before the younger Bliss returned to his father's company, both due to his financial difficulties and Elisha's declining health.

A Tramp Abroad was published in March 1880, and Elisha Bliss died that fall, on September 28. After his death, Clemens had the opportunity to examine some of the financial records pertaining to his books, and concluded that Bliss had cheated him. He sold his stock in the American Publishing Co., and did not publish another book with them for fourteen years— after the competing subscription house that Clemens founded, Charles L. Webster & Co., had ended in bankruptcy.[133]

The present copy of *A Tramp Abroad* bears a pencil note indicating that it originated in the library of Frank Bliss, its would-be publisher.

85⏌ SAMUEL L. CLEMENS, EDMUND CLARENCE STEDMAN, AND FREDERICK J. HALL. Annotated galley proof from *A Connecticut Yankee in King Arthur's Court*. [N.p.], November [1889]. 2 pages, 8½″ x 7″. Published in part: Bucci, Richard. "Mind and Textual Matter." *Studies in Bibliography* 58 (2007): 44.

[The printed phrases "Disembowel me this" and "convey his kidneys" are underlined, and a question mark written in the margin.]

[In Twain's hand, left margin:]

> Dear Mr. Hall:
> Submit this sentence (underlined by Howells,) to Stedman. I strenu-
> ously object to modifying it—in fact ∧ it is already modified, for the
> man would have said guts—but if Stedman sides with Howells I will
> yield. In that case, return it to me for alteration. SLC

[In the hand of Edmund Clarence Stedman, lower left margin:]

> Cleave ~~eleft~~ me this knave in Twain, & convey his lights(?) to ~~the~~ the
> base-born hind his, etc.

[In Twain's hand, right margin:]

> Howells writes: "Last night I read your last chapter of the whole
> book, it's Titanic."

---

133. See Hill, *Mark Twain and Elisha Bliss*, p. 152–158.

Leaves of Grass

405

As I Sat alone
~~Wander'd~~ Ontario
Shores. ~~alone~~ ~~at Night~~

As I Sat alone by
~~wander'd~~ Ontario's
shores alone, ~~at Night~~

As I mused of these mighty
days, and of peace return'd
and the dead that return no
more;
A Phantom, gigantic, superb,
with stern visage, *accosted* arrested me,
Chant me ~~All for Poets~~ yet
a poem, it said, ~~for~~
that the they breathe my
~~breathing~~ ~~my~~ native air alone,
And
Chant me before you go a song of the throes
of Democracy.

2 (Democracy, the destin'd conqueror
— yet treacherous lip-smiles
every where,
And death & infidelity — at every
step.)

PLATE 13.
71] Walt Whitman. Autograph manuscript fragments from "By Blue Ontario's Shore."

Contents

PREFACE. =

~~Introductory Passage~~

~~Hadleyburg Etc~~

1. My Watch — an Instructive little Tale.

2. Political Economy.

3. The Jumping Frog.

4. Journalism in Tennessee.

5. Story of the Bad Little Boy.

6. " " " Good " "

7. Two Poems — by Moore + Twain.

8. A Visit to Niagara.

9. Answers to Correspondents.

10. To Raise Poultry.

PLATE 14.
81] Samuel L. Clemens. Autograph manuscript table of contents for *Mark Twain's Sketches, New and Old*, page 1 of 9.

...quiet my con-

...the knights:

> To the Honorable the Commander of the Insurgent Chivalry of England: You fight in vain. We know your strength—if one may call it by that name. We know

558   *BATTLE OF THE SAND-BELT.*

that at the utmost you cannot bring against us above five and twenty thousand knights. Therefore, you have no chance—none whatever. Reflect: we are well equipped, well fortified, we number 54. Fifty-four what? Men? No, *minds*—the capablest in the world; a force against which mere animal might may no more hope to prevail than may the idle waves of the sea hope to prevail against the granite barriers of England. Be advised. We offer you your lives; for the sake of your families, do not reject the gift. We offer you this chance, and it is the last: throw down your arms; surrender unconditionally to the Republic, and all will be forgiven.

(Signed).   THE BOSS.

I read it to Clarence, and said I proposed to send it by a flag of truce. He laughed the sarcastic laugh he was born with, and said:

"Somehow it seems impossible for you to ever fully realize what these nobilities are. Now let us save a little time and trouble. Consider me the commander of the knights yonder. Now then, you are the flag of truce; approach and deliver me your message, and I will give you your answer."

I humored the idea. I came forward under an imaginary guard of the enemy's soldiers, produced my paper, and read it through. For answer, Clarence struck the paper out of my hand, pursed up a scornful lip and said with lofty disdain—

"Disembowel me this animal, and convey his kidneys to the base-born knave, his master; other answer have I none!"

How empty is theory in presence of fact! And this was just fact, and nothing else. It was the thing that would have happened, there was no getting around that. I tore up the paper and granted my mistimed sentimentalities a permanent rest.

Then, to business. I tested the electric signals from the gatling platform to the cave, and made sure that they were all right; I tested and re-tested those which commanded the fences—these were signals whereby I could break and renew the electric current in each fence independently of the others, at will. I placed the brook-connection under the guard and authority of three of my best boys, who would alternate in two-hour watches all night and promptly obey my signal,

BATTLE OF THE SAND-BELT.

if you had...

PLATE 15.
85] Samuel L. Clemens, Edmund Clarence Stedman, and Frederick J. Hall. Annotated galley proof from *A Connecticut Yankee in King Arthur's Court* (recto).

Mr. Stedman says that this is stronger as it is, but that it had better be changed, he suggests the words "Disembowel" & "Kidney" might offend some.

Dear Mr. Hall:
I yield. Make it read this:
"Dismember me this animal, & return him in a basket to the base-born knave his master; other answer have I none!"

SLC

Nov. 14.

PLATE 16.
85] Samuel L. Clemens, Edmund Clarence Stedman, and Frederick J. Hall. Annotated galley proof from *A Connecticut Yankee in King Arthur's Court* (verso).

[On verso, penciled note in the hand of Frederick J. Hall:]

> Mr. Stedman says that this is stronger as it is, but that it had better be changed, he suggests the words "Disembowel" & "kidneys" might offend some.
> CFW & CE

[In Twain's hand:]

> Dear Mr. Hall:
>   I yield. Make it read thus:
>   "Dismember me this animal, & return him in a basket to the base-born knave his master; other answer I have none!"
> SLC
>   Nov. 14

One of the books issued by Clemens's own subscription house, Charles L. Webster & Co., was *A Connecticut Yankee in King Arthur's Court*. This annotated galley proof of page 558 (plates 15-16) shows a significant amount of discussion of a single sentence in the text. In the proof, the character Clarence states: "Disembowel me this animal, and convey his kidneys to the base-born knave, his master; other answer, I have none!" The marginal annotations surrounding this section show communication between Clemens, his fellow authors and editors W. D. Howells and E. C. Stedman, and Frederick J. Hall, managing editor of the Charles L. Webster Co. Howells identified this sentence as potentially offensive to some readers, and Stedman and Hall seem to have agreed. Clemens's ultimate capitulation to his editors' wishes appears on the verso of the page, and the altered sentence given here appeared in the first American edition of the book. (The sentence appeared in its original, more graphic form in the English edition).

This back-and-forth between the author, his editors, and his friends illuminates Clemens's authorial and editorial process. He had submitted the work to Howells and Stedman for comment, but he also shows a certain protectiveness over the language of his work as he had written it. Twain may have been particularly sensitive to the public's reaction to coarse language: *The Adventures of Huckleberry Finn*, issued five years before, received fierce denunciations from some of its early readers, one of whom declared: "While I do not wish to state it as my opinion that the book is absolutely immoral in its tone, it seems to me that it contains very little humor, and that little is of a coarse type . . . I regard it as the veriest trash."[134]

Richard Bucci notes that the exchange over this sentence in *Connecticut Yankee* illustrates Clemens's powerful position in the editorial process. Unlike other authors, "He could take or leave requests coming from the publishing house, Charles L. Webster, because he was its senior partner . . . The author was more or less at liberty to follow his own artistic lights, but knowing that in places these burned too brightly for the times, was willing to accept moderating advice from trusted sources in the matter of potent words and phrases."[135]

134. Quoted in Hugh Rawson, "Mark Twain's Language: 'Bad' Words Then and Now". *The Huffington Post.* 19 Feb. 2016. Online. < http://www.huffingtonpost.com/hughrawson/mark-twains-language-bad-_b_813459.html > (accessed May 8, 2017).
135. Richard Bucci, "Mind and Textual Matter," *Studies in Bibliography* 58 (2008 2007): 45.

5] [Samuel L. Clemens]. Joseph Keppler. Mark Twain: America's Best Humorist.

Authors of the United States

1]	George Dennison Prentice		22]	Henry Ward Beecher
2]	George Wilkins Kendall		23]	George William Curtis
3]	Alice Cary		24]	Ralph Waldo Emerson
4]	Frederick Swartwout Cozzens		25]	James Russell Lowell
5]	William Davis Gallagher		26]	George Henry Boker
6]	Amelia B. Welby		27]	Bayard Taylor
7]	Richard Henry Stoddard		28]	John Godfrey Saxe
8]	Oliver Wendell Holmes		29]	Lydia Huntley Sigourney
9]	Nathaniel Parker Willis		30]	E.D.E.N. Southworth
10]	George Pope Morris		31]	Catharine Maria Sedgwick
11]	Edgar Allan Poe		32]	Donald Grant Mitchell
12]	Henry Theodore Tuckerman		33]	Henry Wadsworth Longfellow
13]	Nathaniel Hawthorne		34]	William Cullen Bryant
14]	William Gilmore Simms		35]	Fitz-Greene Halleck
15]	Philip Pendelton Cooke		36]	Washington Irving
16]	Charles Fenno Hoffman		37]	Richard Henry Dana
17]	James Fenimore Cooper		38]	Margaret Fuller
18]	William Hickling Prescott		39]	William Ellery Channing
19]	George Bancroft		40]	Harriet Beecher Stowe
20]	Parke Godwin		41]	Caroline Kirkland
21]	John Lothrop Motley		42]	John Greenleaf Whittier

Our Great Authors, A Literary Party at the Home of Washington Irving

1]	Nathaniel Hawthorne		10]	James Russell Lowell
2]	William Gilmore Simms		11]	Nathaniel Parker Willis
3]	Henry Theodore Tuckerman		12]	Henry Wadsworth Longfellow
4]	John Greenleaf Whittier		13]	John Lothrop Motley (?)
5]	John Pendleton Kennedy		14]	Washington Irving
6]	Lewis Gaylord Clark		15]	William Cullen Bryant
7]	Oliver Wendell Holmes		16]	James Fenimore Cooper
8]	William Hickling Prescott		17]	Fitz-Greene Halleck
9]	Ralph Waldo Emerson		18]	George Bancroft

COVER IMAGE: Thomas Hicks (artist), Alexander Hay Ritchie (engraver).
Authors of the United States (item 1).

FRONTISPIECE: [Thomas Sinclair (lithographer)], Pierre Duchochois (photographer).
Our Great Authors, A Literary Party at the Home of Washington Irving (item 2).

*Typeset in
Miller & Bell types.
Printed on Mohawk Vellum and
Neenah Classic Laid papers.
Design & typography
by Jerry Kelly.*